AFTER EDEN

AFTER EDEN

Understanding Creation, the Curse, and the Cross

HENRY MORRIS III
edited by JOHN MORRIS
& HENRY M. MORRIS

First printing: November 2003

ISBN: 0-89051-402-X
Library of Congress Number: 2003106348

Printed in the United States of America

Please visit our website for other great titles:
www.masterbooks.net

For information regarding author interviews,
please contact the publicity department at (870) 438-5288.

Acknowledgments

Having a great heritage is a priceless gift. I am honored to bear the name of Henry M. Morris and to have sat at his feet as his son, a co-worker, and a friend. Much of what is in this book comes indirectly from his legacy. My brother, Dr. John Morris, now president of the Institute for Creation Research, is a contributing editor for this effort and a well-known author and explorer in his own right. These gifts are part of this work.

I am especially grateful to Dr. Gary Parker for his extensive editing contributions and insightful recommendations. Dr. Parker's succinct and straightforward communication style was most helpful in bringing this project to fruition.

Dr. Eugene Merrill, whose text book I used in undergraduate school, was most gracious with his foreword and in his encouragement to maintain a commitment to the authority of God's inspired Word. I am thankful for his comfort. The ICR administrative staff has been especially accommodating. Mark Rasche served as managing editor, coordinating the very proficient editing and proofreading team of Beth Wiles, Debbie Brooks, Greta Forman, and Cheryl Maggio, all in record time. Encouragement has come from all over ICR.

Jan, my dear wife of nearly 40 years, has shared my struggles, labored with me in prayer, and patiently encouraged during the "dry" times. She says that's "just her job," but I know better. Carol Frankenberger, a dear lady in my church, took the raw chapters as they came tumbling out of my computer, and gave her "layman's" feedback with grace and keen insights. Many friends have prayed with my wife and me that God would use this book's challenge for His glory. We all await His answer.

Contents

Foreword

No child spawned by the Eighteenth Century Enlightenment has so effectively infused and, indeed, shaped modern life and thought as naturalistic evolutionism. Best known, perhaps, as the guiding principle of the life sciences, the evolutionary hypothesis has also become the framework within which virtually every other modern area of thought is understood and articulated, including the study of religion.

While it is lamentable, it should not be surprising that the "natural man," as Paul describes him (1 Cor. 2:14), has embraced the evolutionary world view, for with the rejection of the God of the Bible as the sufficient and efficient cause of all things, the most appealing and self-consistent alternative is the evolutionary model. Granting its fundamental presuppositional premises, this model seems better able to explain origins, processes, and results than any other. But it is the granting of these premises that is the sticking point, or at least it ought to be for the Christian who claims to base his epistemological as well as spiritual authority on the Bible, the inerrant and infallible Word of God. The reason for the current dilemma is clear: naturalistic evolutionism and biblical revelation, when both are clearly understood, are essentially contradictory and mutually exclusive.

One might relegate the whole issue of biblical creationism to a marginal area of discussion amongst those who have special interest in such details were it not for the fact that the biblical message itself is rooted and grounded in a theology of creation. God's purpose for the universe in general and more specifically for the human race finds its source in texts that speak of creation as a divine act occurring once, at one moment, and in full development (Gen. 1:1–2:3). No straightforward literary, grammatical, and cultural hermeneutic can yield any other conclusion than that the creation narratives present God as Creator of all things who, by the spoken word, brought them into existence fully mature. The message of the gospel is that Christ came to restore humankind and, indeed, the whole universe to its pristine pre-Fall condition, and the eschatological hope of the world is that it will be recreated to the perfection that God brought to pass in its original state. The recreation will be instantaneous — not the product of eons of development — and thus will match, in short, the first creation as bookends on both sides of history. A sound view of creation, then, is essential to a sound biblical theology.

Because of the apparently irrefutable case made by modern science for the evolutionary hypothesis, many well-intentioned Christians who want to be intellectually respectable and yet hold fast to biblical authority find themselves in a quandary. How can they be true to the text and yet not be marginalized in a culture that understands all reality in evolutionary terms? The answer all too often has been to resort to the expedient of what Morris in this work describes as a "hybrid" evolutionism, an accommodation to the perceived scientific data that is variously described as "theistic evolution," the "gap hypothesis," the "long day" theory, the "day-age" view, "intelligent design," and progressive creationism, among others. There can be no doubt that those who adopt such models do so as devout and sincere brothers and sisters in Christ. But are such compromises necessary or — more bluntly — are they appropriate? Can an ordinary hermeneutic that takes the text at face value not be satisfying to both science and theology when both are methodologically sound and when both bow in humble reverence before the God of the Word and of the world? I think so. This book makes this case and in language and a spirit that are winsome and wise.

Eugene Merrill, Ph.D.
Distinguished Professor
of Old Testament Studies
Dallas Theological Seminary

PREFACE

BY WHOSE AUTHORITY?

What went wrong? "Old timers" in the church can tell you about a time when school boards and city councils would NOT want to offend the ministerium, or local group of pastors. It was not the pastors' academic degrees, rhetorical skills, financial clout, or threats of lawsuits that earned their respect. Instead, the pastors brought the Bible to bear on the human condition, and the clear and compelling Word of God was their source of respect and authority.

Today, if a pastor dares to preach a biblical message on abstinence, homosexuality, or the roles of husband and wife in the family, he is likely to be denounced by a plethora of Christian leaders as ignorant, intolerant, unloving, and out of touch. If a group of Christian parents approach their school board to ask for fair treatment of creation when evolution is taught, they will likely encounter condescension or open ridicule.

What has changed?

The authority of God's Word has been replaced by the authority of human opinion. In many churches, Christian colleges, and seminaries, the diluting down of biblical authority has been led by those who want to hybridize Scripture with the "more scientifically acceptable" view of long ages of death and struggle.

The National Center for Science Education (NCSE) was formed to ban creation from our public classrooms. Should students ask about creation, the NCSE recommend that teachers simply tell the students to ask their pastors or clergymen — knowing that, in most cases, their pastors will tell students it is okay to accept evolution. The sad part about that strategy is that it works very well!

Why does it work? After two decades of losing scientific debates to creationists, its seems that evolutionists realized that they might be more effective by using respected and popular Christian leaders to undermine belief in the biblical record of earth's history. The minimum requirement for evolution is long ages of death and struggle, and many mainstream Christian leaders willingly accommodate that. Some just say God used evolution; others put long ages of death and struggle between Lucifer's rebellion and Adam's sin. The favorites of evolutionists, however, are Christian compromises, such as progressive creation, that maximize confusion about the meaning of the creation days and minimize the effects on the world of man's sin and God's judgment at Noah's flood.

An eloquent speaker who is both a scientist and a professing Christian, Dr. Hugh Ross is recognized as a major leader in the movement to find a place for long ages of death and struggle in the biblical account. He believes they belong in a creation "week" of billions of years, that predators were killing and eating live animals long before Adam's sin, and that Noah's "universal" flood filled only the Mesopotamian valley. Deadlier still, he believes that these beliefs can be supported by a "scholarly interpretation" of Scripture that uses nature as a "67th book of the Bible" to tell us what Genesis 1–11 really means.

It is no wonder that Eugenie Scott, head of the anti-creationist agency mentioned earlier and self-described "philosophical materialist" (i.e., atheist), concedes to Hugh Ross's approach to creation/evolution: Ross "does reflect a lot of mainstream science in his views . . . others feel he is making a contribution in helping conservative Christians embrace more science."[1] Although this example goes beyond the case just cited, one would certainly wonder about any church's evangelism program if it were endorsed by the national atheist society!

Having not had to compromise at all, evolutionists can eagerly accept the view of Christian leaders who find support for long ages of death and struggle in the Bible. For them, it means that human opinion reigns supreme. When the arguments for

Christian compromise in this generation pass into the dust bin of history, long ages of death and struggle will still be standing as the absolute certainty, as evolutionists see it, and a new generation of "Christian scholars" will find new ways to bend the Bible to fit with it.

Remember Paul and the Berean Church? Paul is acknowledged as a true intellectual giant, and he could have awed the Bereans with "great swelling words." But Paul resolved "not to know any thing among you, save Jesus Christ, and him crucified" (1 Cor. 2:2). This is the same Paul who elsewhere feared that the Corinthians' "minds [would] be corrupted from the simplicity that is in Christ" (2 Cor. 11:3). The first lesson is as clear as the words Paul used: Christian leaders who want to honor God and to build up His church will speak clearly and plainly, just as Jesus did, wanting God's message to be understood and applied.

The second lesson comes from the Bereans' response. They could have been awed by Paul's credentials and intellectual prowess, but they were not. They *"searched the scriptures daily, [to see if] those things were so"* (Acts 17:11). Berean laymen assumed it was their duty to check out the expert. Could they argue with him over the nuances of Hebrew verb tenses or the cultural context surrounding a prophecy? Probably not. However, using the clear and simple words God inspired, they could see if he was building his case on the sure foundation of God's Word!

How can Christians establish the authority of the never-changing Word of God over the ever-changing words of men? For Christian leaders, that means preaching and teaching God's Word just as He so clearly and carefully inspired it. For Christian laymen, that means checking out the "experts," making sure the words of those experts are rooted in those words God has caused to be written — so simply that even a child can understand.

The initial chapters of this book outline the intellectual hybrids that mix the message of God and the facts of nature with atheistic explanations, especially long ages of death and struggle. The next part demonstrates the precision with which we are expected to use the Scriptures and contains a review of the textual data that covers the record of Creation, the Fall of man, and the flood of Noah. Emphasis is on the tight demand that language places on readers, especially when the language is given by the inspiration of an omniscient Creator.

The final chapters then point out the false logic and false science behind the hybrid proposals. A conscious effort has been made to expose the fallacies of the arguments. They also address the impact that the hybrid arguments have made on the Church at large and how damaging these arguments can be to individual faith and trust in the words and work of the Lord Jesus.

Both Christian leaders and Christian laymen are encouraged to resist the undermining of Scripture and to return to a confident trust in what God has caused to be recorded.

Endnotes

1 Andy Butcher, "He Sees God in the Stars" (includes an interview with Eugenie Scott), in *Charisma and Christian Life*, June 2003, p. 38–44.

Chapter 1

Two Gates

On no account must you look at the great mob, but only at the Word of God.[1]

— Martin Luther

Charles Templeton had a dramatic bedside conversion when he was a young man, was ordained in the Church of the Nazarene, and became the minister of Avenue Road Church in Toronto and a widely effective evangelist with Youth for Christ. He served as secretary of evangelism for the National Council of Churches of Christ, U.S.A., and director of evangelism for the Presbyterian Church, USA. For nearly 20 years, Charles Templeton preached the gospel and promoted the Christian life in pulpits, stadiums, and universities and on the weekly CBS television program "Look Up and Live." By all outward appearances, he was a dynamic, passionate, and genuinely committed believer.

Unfortunately, all was not well inside.

In his last book, appropriately titled *Farewell to God*, Charles Templeton discloses his life story, tells of his double-minded struggle during the years of his ministry, and relates the intellectual battle that began to pull him further and further away from Scripture. Chapter after chapter derides the idea of a personal God, attacks the concept of an inspired Bible, denigrates the person of Jesus Christ, lambastes the church, preachers of the gospel, the Christian treatment of women, and the whole idea of good and evil. In Templeton's final summary of his belief system, the "I Believe" credo, he writes:

> I believe that there is no supreme being with human attributes — no God in the biblical sense — but that all life is the result of timeless evolutionary forces, having reached its present transient state over millions of years.[2]

How did such a startling change occur? Why did Charles Templeton change from an active ministry as a soul-winning evangelist to a committed non-believer? Perhaps the answers lie in the account of his personal friendship with Billy Graham and Charles' intense efforts to dissuade Dr. Graham from an unwavering belief in the Word of God.

> Just before I enrolled at Princeton, we met again in New York City. On this occasion we spent the better part of two days closeted in a room in the Taft Hotel. All our differences came to a head in a discussion. . . . I said, "But, Billy, it's simply not possible any longer to believe, for instance, the biblical account of creation. The world wasn't created over a period of days a few thousand years ago; it has evolved over millions of years. It's not a matter of speculation; it's demonstrable fact."
>
> "I don't accept that," Billy said. "And there are reputable scholars who don't."
>
> "Who are those scholars?" I said. "Men in conservative Christian colleges."
>
> "Most of them, yes," he said. "But that's not the point. I believe the Genesis account of creation because it's in the Bible. I've discovered something in my ministry: when I take the Bible literally, when I proclaim it as the Word of God, my preaching has power. . . . Wiser men than you and I have been arguing questions like this for centuries. I don't have the time or the intellect to examine all sides of each theological dispute, so I've decided, once and for all, to stop questioning and accept the Bible as God's Word."
>
> "But, Billy," I protested, "you can't do that. You don't dare stop thinking about the most important question in life. Do it and you begin to die. It's intellectual suicide."[3]

Charles needed to have a "life of unrestricted thought,"[4] yet he cut himself off from the truth in Christ that would have set him free from the finite limits of merely human knowledge. After the years of inner turmoil, he left the ministry, denounced his faith, and became an active anti-Christian agnostic, publishing several books with the intent to sway the minds of people away from a belief in the message of Scripture. The Bible, he insisted, is "not the revealed word of a deity but the conclusions and insights of men and women who, across the centuries, have sought to understand and explain the mysteries of existence."[5] Charles Templeton was unwilling to have his mind submitted to any authority but his own. "Surely," he says,

> As we approach the twenty-first century it is time to have done with primitive speculation and superstition and look at life in rational terms. We are in large measure the masters of our fate — subject, of course, to our genetic inheritance, mental illness, accident, or disease — and we are all equipped to ponder the eternal questions, explore the unknown, and examine the *mysterium tremendum* secure in the knowledge that in doing so we are not going counter to "the will of God" and will not bring on ourselves the vengeful wrath of some punctilious deity because we rejected or failed to observe some arcane prohibition.[6]

It is obvious that Billy Graham chose one way and Charles Templeton chose another. Both men were intellectually honest. Both of them reached the logical conclusions of their presuppositions. How *very* different were their conclusions! That fateful conversation demonstrates the importance of starting points, presuppositions, and the basis for assessing truth. Where one ends often depends critically upon where one begins.

Two Spiritual Gates Open Different Eternal Destinies

Jesus teaches that there is a narrow gate and a wide gate (Matt. 7:13–14) that open onto different roads. The narrow gate is difficult to go through (Luke 13:24) and has few entrants, but the wide gate opens onto a broad road that many take. These two gates lead to very different places according to the Lord Jesus Christ. One leads to eternal life while the other leads to destruction. Many attempts have been made to confuse the two roads — or to insist that both roads really lead to the same place. The gleeful and confident majority always tries to justify its decision to saunter down the broad road and frequently make fun of the minority who chooses to enter the narrow gate. Unfortunately, few today make an effort to point out the different gates and the quite different destinations!

Jesus Claims To BE the Narrow Gate

The words of Scripture declare that Jesus *is* the narrow gate:

- Jesus saith unto him, I am the way, the truth, and the life: no man cometh unto the Father, but by me (John 14:6).
- Then said Jesus unto them again, Verily, verily, I say unto you, I am the door of the sheep. . . . I am the door: by me if any man enter in, he shall be saved, and shall go in and out, and find pasture (John 10:7–9).
- Jesus said unto her, I am the resurrection, and the life. . . . Believest thou this? (John 11:25–26).

We have the ability to reject His claims, of course — Adam and Eve did at one point, and so did Charles Templeton. Whether we reject it or not, it would be ridiculous to say that Jesus did not claim to be the narrow gate. If Jesus *is* who He claims to be, then the gate is very narrow indeed. So narrow in fact, that the Bible says no man or woman can see the gate without supernatural help from God!

We Need God's Help To Find the Narrow Gate

When Jesus officially started his public ministry, he read the following portion from the scroll of Isaiah to the synagogue leaders in Nazareth:

> The Spirit of the Lord is upon me, because he hath anointed me to preach the gospel to the poor; he hath sent me to heal the brokenhearted, to preach deliverance to the captives, and recovering of sight to the blind, to set at liberty them that are bruised, to preach the acceptable year of the Lord (Luke 4:18–19).

Jesus also said, "No man can come to me, except the Father which hath sent me draw him: and I will raise him up at the last day" (John 6:44). Paul the Apostle preached the same message when he told King Agrippa what God had called him to do:

> Now I [Jesus] send thee, to open their eyes, and to turn them from darkness to light, and from the power of Satan unto God, that they may receive forgiveness of sins, and inheritance among them which are sanctified by faith that is in me (Acts 26:17–18).

We are not going to find that narrow gate without God's help.

Only the Teachings of Jesus Christ Reveal the Narrow Gate

Jesus also insisted that His words were the only words that would lead us to the narrow gate (himself) and through that gate to eternal life.

- Verily, verily, I say unto you, He that heareth my word, and believeth on him that sent me, hath everlasting life, and shall not come into condemnation; but is passed from death unto life (John 5:24).
- Jesus answered them, and said, My doctrine is not mine, but his that sent me. If any man will do his will, he shall know of the doctrine, whether it be of God, or whether I speak of myself (John 7:16–17).
- And ye shall know the truth, and the truth shall make you free (John 8:32).
- And I, if I be lifted up from the earth, will draw all men unto me (John 12:32).

- Sanctify them through thy truth: thy word is truth (John 17:17).

We will never find the gate that leads to eternal life unless we pay attention to the words that God has spoken to us through His Son, Jesus (Heb. 1:1–3; 2:1–4).

The Wide Gate Is also Impossible To See — Apart from Scripture

Tammy Bruce, a lesbian from age 17 and involved in the gay rights movement for many years, became president of the Los Angeles chapter of the National Organization for Women. Tammy, active in ultra-left politics and gay feminist agendas, was committed to the pro-choice lobby "primarily because of [her] skewed vision of right and wrong and [her] willingness to enter a world swirling around a moral vacuum."[7]

Part of the dilemma faced by Tammy and many others is that *neither* gate is visible to the *natural* eye. The narrow gate is hard to find because Jesus is the only way through it. The wide gate is so vast that we are not aware of being in it. It is like standing on the floor of a huge river valley — the sides are so far away that the valley itself cannot be seen.

The wide gate is invisible because whole cities and entire nations fit inside the gate. This gate does not look like a gate at all — it looks like what everybody else is doing!

- There is a way which seemeth right unto a man, but the end thereof are the ways of death (Prov. 14:12).
- But the natural man receiveth not the things of the Spirit of God: for they are foolishness unto him: neither can he know them, because they are spiritually discerned (1 Cor. 2:14).

The reliance on our own thinking seems to be the crux of the Bible's warnings. Natural thinking, the human *intellect* with which we are born, has been *corrupted* and cannot find the way to the narrow gate. To find the gate, we need the supernatural intervention of the Spirit of God through the ministry of the Lord Jesus

(Isa. 42:5–7; Luke 4:18–19). At sometime in life, every intellectually cogent man and woman is faced with the sight of the narrow gate (John 6:44; 12:32). Some rejoice at the sight and begin their journey to eternal life. Others waffle and delay, ultimately rejecting the narrow gate in favor of the wide gate, and continue on their road to destruction (Rom. 1:20–32).

Still others, like Tammy Bruce, go a long way down the broad road only to find that their companions have become terribly distasteful. They start to look around for the other road. What brought about *this* change? Tammy certainly does not suggest that she has had anything like a conversion of faith. She even takes careful pains to make it clear that she is not a Christian. What happened then? What caused her to switch from reveling in a very liberal and openly decadent lifestyle to becoming a proponent of conservative ethics and morals?

"You don't, after all," Tammy says, "need to be steeped in religious fundamentalism to realize things have gone terribly wrong. . . . Faith, family, fidelity, truth, and honor all became casualties of America's Cultural Elite."[8] After living in some of the deepest stench of the broad road, Tammy Bruce began to understand that "the disintegration of our culture, and the conditioning of people into accepting it in silence, begins with legitimizing the depraved."[9] She also saw that "without rules, there is no perspective, no right and wrong — only relativism, and a culture of self-gratification where everyone loses, especially the generation that must inherit our folly."[10]

Good insight! That is exactly what God says. The human race is depraved and must have rules enforced by those that God delegates to carry out His rules (Rom. 13:1–4). Tammy does not believe in a personal God — yet. What she does embrace is the rules of people who believe in God — more or less.

> I don't identify myself as a Christian, and yet, like the average person, I recognize the extraordinary value of the most basic personal ethics enshrined in the Judeo-Christian tradition. . . . The personal standards it encourages do not impinge on the quality of life, but enhance it.[11]

> The challenge for us is to be able to be true to our principles, while recognizing the humanity of those who disagree with us. . . . We can instead do our best to live honest lives, replete with the discomfort of shame, the difficulties of personal responsibility, and the joy, the genuine happiness, that only right and good can bring. We will, in the end, have the reward of being better people.[12]

Well, that is nice, but just how does she arrive at that set of conclusions? Why does she pick the rules of the Judeo-Christian tradition over, say, the Buddhist's ten steps to Nirvana or Deepak Chopra's recipe for well being? Much of what Tammy Bruce endorses would be endorsed by evangelical Christianity. Does that similarity make her the same as a born again believer? Tammy is still in a lesbian relationship. She is still actively pro-choice. She is still picking and choosing the rules that she wants to follow and is merely rationalizing her choice because, in her eyes, the majority of the good people with common sense agree with her.[13]

Tammy may be looking for the narrow gate, but she has not yet found it.

The Choice of Gates Seems To Hinge on How We View the Creation

Charles Templeton, with his knowledge of the narrow gate, appeared to walk through it and embrace the way that leads to life, only then to switch roads with a fierce determination! Tammy Bruce surely has come to understand that only chaos ensues when there are no rules, but she apparently has not yet met the Rule Maker.

- Beware lest any man spoil you through philosophy and vain deceit, after the tradition of men, after the rudiments of the world, and not after Christ (Col. 2:8).
- Let no man beguile you . . . intruding into those things which he hath not seen, vainly puffed up by his fleshly mind (Col. 2:18).

At the age of 15, Dan Barker went forward during a revival service to accept God's call on his life to serve in the ministry. Twenty years later, he wrote the following in a letter to an editor of *Freethought Today*, a publication of the Freedom From Religion Foundation:

> I was a minister for a number of years . . . and I used to proudly wave the Bible as the only standard for humanity. I have just emerged from a painful five year process of conversion from Christianity to atheism. . . . I spent years in evangelism, missions, and Christian music. I wrote two popular Christian musicals which are still being performed around the world. Now that I have left Christianity I still feel the energy to make a kind of contribution to values and intelligence.[14]

Today, Dan Barker is the public relations director of the Freedom From Religion Foundation and speaks all over the country challenging anyone who will debate him. He brags that he is "no puppet of a higher mind, no slave to eternity."[15]

What brought about this radical transformation? Did Dan Barker hate God in some unusual way? How could such a thing happen? More appropriate to the issues discussed in this book, what is the common denominator between Charles Templeton and Dan Barker? Why did they reject their faith in the God of creation? How could seemingly good men go bad? Apparently, both began by taking small intellectual steps away from the faith — beginning with distrust in the historicity of the biblical account of creation. Charles said, "I had always doubted the Genesis account of creation and could never accept the monstrous evil of an endless hell."[16] In a similar manner, Dan Barker recounted his own stepwise fall from faith in his book *Losing Faith in Faith*:

> I used to believe that Adam and Eve were literal. . . . But I got to thinking that there are parts of the Bible that are obviously metaphorical. . . . The Garden of Eden could have been a Hebrew "parable" to explain

> God's involvement with the human race regarding origins, good and evil. . . . My first tiny step away from fundamentalism was . . . to realize that it shouldn't matter to me whether other Christians held it historically. . . . Sounds silly, but that was a big step in the direction of tolerance. . . .
>
> After a couple of years I migrated further into a more moderate position . . . but discarded many lesser doctrines as either nonessential, or untrue. . . .
>
> The line that I was drawing . . . kept rising until it popped right off the top of the list! To my list of religious metaphors, which included the Prodigal Son and Adam and Eve, I now added God. That made perfect sense.[17]

Both Dan Barker's and Charles Templeton's books are recent examples of similar books written over the centuries. Most books like theirs present intellectual arguments for an anti-God, anti-Bible, anti-Christian lifestyle. In every case, the foundational argument seems to be that the creation record of the Bible is not accurate and that evidence — whether scientific or experiential — proves that God either does not exist or, if such a "thing" does pervade the universe, "it" is detached and uninvolved in the affairs of men.

What about Tammy Bruce? She is trying to find stability and order in a world that has rapidly become more disgustingly tolerant of anything and everything except the rules of God. Why is it that her halfway measures cannot work and will not ultimately satisfy? Why do many listen to her plea for goodness but go right on doing what they want to do anyway? After years of productive ministry, why did Charles Templeton and Dan Barker reject God and faith in Christ? Where does a true change start? What is the foundation from which order and purpose can flow?

The answer to any of these questions lies in the answer to *the* foundational question: "On what basis is truth to be determined? Is it the never-changing Word of God, or the ever-changing words of men?"

Creation — Literal Reading or Interpretation?

Dan Barker and Charles Templeton did not begin their repudiation of the Christian faith by rejecting John 3:16, Christ's love, or the hope of heaven. It began, as Dan Barker described it himself, when he ceased to take the account of Adam and Eve and the Garden literally. Instead of seeing biblical history as real history, he began to interpret it as religious metaphor, and that literary framework progressed through Scripture until, as he tells us, he finally "added God" to his "list of religious metaphors."

Charles Templeton was just as clear. In his conversation with Billy Graham, Charles Templeton justified his rejection of the Bible as God's Word because, in his words, "The world wasn't created over a period of days a few thousand years ago; it has evolved over millions of years."[18] Templeton deliberately chose to base his beliefs about origins (and, hence, his answers to all other questions) on the words of men, not the Word of God. Billy Graham made the opposite choice. Why? In Billy's words, "I believe the Genesis account of creation because it's in the Bible."[19]

If one takes God at His Word, accepting the meaning of words and sentences as determined by grammar and context, *one reads* (not interpreting) God's Word literally. Taking God literally means, of course, that the parables are taken as parables, poetry as poetry, visions as visions, metaphors as metaphors, figurative language as figurative language, commandments as commandments, and history as history. The foundational belief of the literalist is that the Bible is God's revelation, a revealing of himself, so God wants to speak clearly, and be clearly understood, by those who accept Him with the trusting faith and the desire to learn of a loving child.

If a passage is not clear to us, we are to compare it with other passages in Scripture. As the old hymn puts it, "God is His own Interpreter, and He will make it plain."[20] If someone insists on calling a literal reading an interpretation, then let it be called the scriptural interpretation of Scripture, biblical interpretation, or internal interpretation — letting God use His own inspired words to communicate His own inspired meaning.

Those who seek to fit long ages of death and struggle into the biblical narrative must use the word *interpretation* to mean something quite different from the understanding and application of God's words taken clearly and simply (literally) in God's context. Even those who think the concepts are allegorical or mythical freely admit that — if God said what He meant and meant what He said — Genesis 1–11 would be read by any intelligent person of any time or any culture as teaching that God created the heavens and the earth in six ordinary days; that man's sin brought death and struggle into the world that God had created very good; and that God used a mountain-covering Flood that rose and fell over many months to destroy all air-breathing land life except those with Noah in the ark. That simple, direct reading and understanding is confirmed many other places in Scriptures and in the words of Jesus himself.

Given an account so clear and concise, so direct and dramatic, so pregnant with purpose and majestic in meaning, what options exist for its meaning?

First, one can accept the account as written (i.e., take it literally), and apply it to build an understanding of humanity, our world, and the universe. That approach is taken by many scientists, educators, theologians, and other Christian leaders and laymen. Basing their work on the historicity of Genesis 1–11, biologists, geologists, and astrophysicists committed to the authority of God's Word have done phenomenal research attracting even grudging respect from secular scientists and anti-creationists!

Second, one can reject the account in Genesis 1–11, reject the God who claims to have inspired it, and reject the Christ who believed and taught it. That is not the response for which a Christian would hope, of course, but at least it is honest. (This is the choice Charles Templeton and Dan Barker made.)

Third, one can reject the account as history and science, but keep it as allegory and embrace a God who would use the account to teach spiritual truths. Such a position, like theistic evolution, usually allows one to keep his standing in the secular community (as long as the "theistic" does not interfere too much with the "evolution").

A fourth option is becoming very popular for those who want to keep a degree of respectability in *both* the secular community *and* the Christian community. Interpret Genesis 1–11 in a way that incorporates *long ages of death and struggle* (the very thing Charles Templeton called the "demonstrable fact" that forced his *Farewell to God*).

Is it possible to interpret Scripture so that it means something other than what the words, grammar, and context suggest? The answer to that question is always "yes" — for the wrong reasons! However, once one moves beyond comparing Scripture with Scripture, the possibilities are limited only by human imagination. The merits of any such human interpretation are judged primarily by the number of followers it attracts.

Such interpretation begins when something outside Scripture — concept, experience, or personal preference — is considered so absolutely certain that, if the biblical text seems inconsistent with it, new meaning must be sought for the Scripture in question. Today, many consider that extra-biblical absolute certainty to be long ages of death and struggle. Charles Templeton concluded "the world . . . evolved over millions of years. It's not a matter of speculation; it's demonstrable fact"; acceptance of that "demonstrable fact" became the basis for interpreting Scripture in a new way, a way that finally led to his rejection of God's Word, and the God who claims to have inspired it.[21]

We will look at various attempts to interpret Scripture to accommodate the "absolute certainty" of long ages of death and struggle in the next chapter. Until then, consider the following questions: After Christians have been convinced that long ages of death and struggle were part of God's perfect creation for millions of years before man's sin, what new meaning will Christ's death have? After accepting that some dinosaurs were tearing others to shreds for millions of years until God wiped them all out with an asteroid, how will Christians answer those who reject the idea of God because they cannot believe an all-powerful, all-loving Creator would be so "cruel, wasteful, and inefficient." If "day" does not mean "day", why would "resurrection" mean "resurrection"? Perhaps resurrection means only that those who do enough good deeds will be lovingly remembered after death — and those who read the Bible with child-like faith "are of all men most miserable" (1 Cor. 15:19).

Ideas Have Consequences

Scientific and philosophical thinkers who enter into the box of evolutionary and naturalistic restrictions are bound to render evolutionary and naturalistic conclusions. If one excludes the possibility of the supernatural, then one is absolutely bound to interpret within the framework of that belief. Whatever the discipline, framework, or presuppositions, the belief system orchestrates both the approach to information and the conclusion drawn from that information. Dr. Francis Schaffer offers this keen insight:

> The basic problem of the Christians in this country in the last 80 years or so, in regard to society and in regard to government, is that they have seen things in bits and pieces instead of totals.
>
> They have very gradually become disturbed over permissiveness, pornography, the public schools, the breakdown of the family, and finally abortion. But they have not seen this as a totality — each thing being a part, a symptom, of a much larger problem. They have failed to see that all of this has come about due to a shift in world view — that is, through a fundamental change in the overall way people think and view the world and life as a whole. This shift has been *away from* a world view that was at least vaguely Christian in people's memory (even if they were not individually Christian) *toward* something completely different — toward a world view based upon the idea that the final reality is impersonal

> matter or energy shaped into its present form by impersonal chance. They have not seen that this world view has taken the place of the one that had previously dominated Northern European culture, including the United States, which was at least Christian in memory, even if the individuals were not individually Christian.
>
> These two world views stand as totals in complete antithesis to each other in content and also in their natural results — including sociological and governmental results, and specifically including law.
>
> It is not that these two world views are different only in how they understand the nature of reality and existence. They also inevitably produce totally different results. The operative word here is *inevitably*. It is not just that they happen to bring forth different results, but it is absolutely *inevitable* that they will bring forth different results.[22]

It is inevitable that if we begin with different premises, different results will be produced. That is a rather profound thought and one that has demonstrated itself in recent years by the agonizing efforts of Christian writers to somehow resolve the differences between two vastly different world views.

Belief Systems Control Your Life

Dr. Dallas Willard gives another perspective on the same issue:

> And here also is one of those points where the educational practices that have developed in our society deeply injure our souls and impede the coming of the kingdom into our lives. In our culture one is considered educated if one "knows the right answers." That is, if one knows which answers are the correct ones. I sometimes joke with my students at the university where I teach by asking them if they believe what they wrote on their tests. They always laugh. They know belief is not required. Belief only controls your life.[23]

"Belief only controls your life." This idea is perhaps the crux of the matter. Often, students are trained to produce the "right" (correct) answers throughout their education — answers that match the presuppositions of their teachers and their textbooks. That training encourages students to embrace the information presented to them without question. The conflict comes when the concept taught collides with the faith believed. Cloaking itself in the garb of scientific jargon, philosophic naturalism presents a vastly different view of whom and what we are than do the pages of Scripture. It is not possible that the two belief systems are both true, so we tend to adopt one system and order our lives after its tenets. "No man can serve two masters" (Matt. 6:24).

Dr. Schaeffer describes a shift in world view over the past century. Dr. Willard speaks as a current professor at the University of Southern California's School of Philosophy. Both note the *control* that belief systems have on our lives. Both note the inexorable direction and end results of the opposite ways of thinking.

Strange, is it not, that only the Christian camp has attempted to merge the two opposite philosophies?

Education Has Shifted Focus Over the Centuries

Western civilization grew out of the biblical belief that God created order and purpose, that man's sin corrupted God's creation and brought on the catastrophe of Noah's flood, but that order and purpose could and would be restored through new life in Jesus Christ. In the 1800s, another belief system gained prominence, one based on the twin towers of long ages provided by Charles Lyell's uniformitarianism and one based on death and struggle proposed by Charles Darwin as a mechanism for progressive evolution of ever-more-fit life forms.

The evolutionary framework of long ages of death and struggle replaced the Bible as the pillar and ground of the truth. By the 1900s, God was effectively excluded from erudite conversation. University systems began priding themselves on an open hostility to "religious dogma," and a great cry for "academic freedom" reverberated across the intellectual world. The Bible became a disdained book of legends and myths; religious faith was seen as a hindrance to the search for truth. From a foundation that sought God for insight into truth, Western society had shifted into a period of *questioning* all truth and then entered into an era that now believes that there *is* no absolute truth.

The New Open-minded Tolerance

At a creation/evolution debate in the Miami area, the evolutionist debating was hammering home repeatedly that Einstein showed that all things are relative and that there are no absolutes. Finally the moderator interrupted, "Are you absolutely sure about that?" Even the debater joined the audience's laughter, quipping that he had been "hoisted on his own petard."

The only virtues that seem approved in a society without absolutes are perverse forms of open-mindedness and tolerance. Being open-minded or tolerant originally meant for example, engaging in give-and-take dialog, defending views while listening respectfully to another's, or freely "competing in the marketplace of ideas" — even if the interchange ended by finally and fervently agreeing to disagree. In the brave new world of the politically correct, however, open-mindedness and tolerance mean much more than just granting different views a fair and respectful hearing. Such tolerance means that one must accept any other view as just as valid, or just as true, as one's own. Those who insist on absolutes are labeled intolerant and are thus not tolerated.

The multitudes walking through the broad gate fully grant each other "open-minded toleration," since each of their views is based on nothing higher than human authority. All are united in opposition to those walking through the narrow gate, who are building on biblical authority. The Bible-believer can and should be speaking out in the market place of ideas, "ready always to give an answer to every man that asketh you a reason of the hope that is in you with [gentleness]" (1 Pet. 3:15). Having once been on the broad way, the believer can and should be lovingly open-minded and tolerant — in the original sense of those words. In doing so, the Christian can never consider views based on the words of man as having equal validity with those based on the Word of God; nor can the Christian ever accept another door to eternal reality than the narrow gate, which is Christ himself.

Nothing brings out close-minded intolerance better than the loving, but exclusive, claims of the risen Savior! Charles Templeton and Dan Barker wanted "academic freedom"; but they knew that the Bible taught: "ye shall know the truth, and the truth shall make you free" (John 8:32). That truth had to be rejected to maintain their "freedom" from it.

The living Word of God can lift us far above the finite human limits of time and culture and give us a breathtaking view of eternity from beginning to end and of our place in it. But Templeton and Barker willingly surrendered truth and freedom based on God's Word for truth and freedom based on man's wisdom. Accepting long ages of death and struggle as their view of origins, they chose to put their trust in three pounds of mostly fat (the human brain) supposedly wired by evolution to give man a slight advantage over other primates in the struggle for food and mates. How small indeed is the truthless freedom found in the tiny windowless box of philosophic naturalism.

Yet many pastors, professors, and para-church ministries are encouraging Christians to incorporate long ages of death and struggle into a new interpretation of the biblical message. Man's intellect is now used to explain away the inconsistencies between the biblical text and the doctrines of naturalism. Deconstruction of biblical words has become commonplace, with new systems of theology being generated to promulgate the error. Dynamic translations and culturally relevant editions are replacing scholarly efforts to translate the original texts. God's words have become God's thoughts — musing thoughts that are open to "interpretation" and "relevant application." What is "true for me" in Scripture has become more important than careful linguistic definition or precise words used in context.

Why Are Origins Issues So Important for Christians?

Questions about origins affect our understanding of both God's world and God's Word. Are those two sources of information at odds or in harmony — or is some extra-biblical interpretation required to harmonize them? Do we dare interpret origins in the light of men's words when no human observers were present, or can we fully trust the Word of the God who was there and who told us what He created, how He created, how long He took, how man's sin affected His creation, why Christ's death was necessary, and why Christ's return will usher in new heavens and a new earth? Why, indeed, do the very first words that come from the Creator tell us about His creative work?

- Maybe, without a confidence in God as Creator, we cannot have confidence in God as Savior.
- Maybe, if we doubt God's Word the first time He speaks, we cannot believe Him completely on anything else He says.
- Maybe, if we act as if God is a liar when He tells us what He has done to help us see who He is, He will not show us the narrow gate.
- Maybe, if we try to make Scripture fit evolution's interpretation of science, we will find that true science supports God's Word — literally.

This book contrasts the startlingly different views of two groups of Christians. One group seems to feel that the Christian faith can survive in this post-Christian scientific age only if a place can be found in Scripture for long ages of death and struggle. Literalists, the opposing group, relate death and struggle to biblical teachings of a young earth and sin. Attempts will be made to demonstrate the impact of the opposite positions, the impossibility of trying to hybridize them, and the damage that hybrid views do to the precious gospel of our Lord Jesus Christ.

So then because thou art lukewarm, and neither cold nor hot, I will spue thee out of my mouth (Rev. 3:16).

Endnotes

1 Jaroslav Pelikan, editor, *Martin Luther, Luther's Works,* Vol. 21: *The Sermon on the Mount and the Magnificat* (St Louis, MO: Concordia Publishing House, 1956), p. 243.
2 Charles Templeton, *Farewell to God* (Toronto: McClelland & Stewart Inc., 1996), p. 232.
3 Ibid., p. 7–8.
4 Ibid., p. 9.
5 Ibid., p. 20.
6 Ibid., p. 21.
7 Tammy Bruce, *The Death of Right and Wrong* (Roseville, CA: Prima Publishing, Forum, 2003), p. 7.
8 Ibid., p. 20.
9 Ibid., p. 21.
10 Ibid., p. 35.
11 Ibid.
12 Ibid., p. 293.
13 Ibid., p. 13.
14 Dan Barker, *Losing Faith in Faith* (Madison, WI: Freedom From Religion Foundation, Inc., 1992), p. 9–10.
15 Ibid., p. 228.
16 Templeton, *Farewell to God*, p. 6.
17 Barker, *Losing Faith in Faith*, p. 28–31.
18 Templeton, *Farewell to God*, p. 7.
19 Ibid., p. 7.
20 William Cowper, "Light Shining Out of Darkness," lines 23–24.
21 Templeton, *Farewell to God*, p. 7.
22 Francis A. Schaffer, *A Christian Manifesto* (Westchester, IL: Crossway Books, 1981), rev. ed. 1982, p. 17–18.
23 Dallas Willard, *The Divine Conspiracy: Rediscovering Our Hidden Life in God* (San Francisco, CA: Harper, 1998), p. 317.

Chapter 2

Science Falsely So Called

If our culture is to be transformed, it will happen from the bottom up — from ordinary believers practicing apologetics over the backyard fence or around the barbecue grill. To be sure, it's important for Christian scholars to conduct research and hold academic symposia, but the real leverage for cultural change comes from transforming the habits and dispositions of ordinary people.[1]

— Charles Colson

Few if any people today would want to live without the blessings of modern science. Experimental science has earned our respect and admiration as a superb technique for exploring the wonders of our universe, finding patterns of order, and applying knowledge for the benefit of mankind.

Originally, the word "science" meant something much broader than the experimental or empirical discipline people think of today. In its broad sense, "science" means knowledge and refers both to the organized body of information and concepts produced by human study and to the various techniques of investigation used to acquire such knowledge. Indeed, theology was once called the "Queen of the Sciences," the branch of science that tied all the other branches together.

Science has a much more restrictive meaning today. It has come to refer specifically to information and concepts discovered and applied through continuous interplay of hypothesis and observation. Concepts are considered scientific if, and only if, they can be tested and refuted or supported (never proven) by repeatable observations. Its dependence on repeatable observations gives experimental science its vaunted objectivity. It is the scientist whose predictions are confirmed by verified observation who wins the argument. Majority vote, rhetorical eloquence, and media endorsement should count for nothing in real science. No less a scientist than Einstein exemplified the true spirit of science when he said that new evidence smashed certain of his theories like a hammer blow.

Science derives its strength from its limits. By restricting its interest to observationally testable concepts, science achieves a degree of objectivity beyond that of other disciplines. By limiting its domain of interest to measurable physical phenomena, pure science skirts questions of ethics and morality that have stalled philosophers for centuries. By seeking only to make and to use statements (scientific theories) that predict the behavior of nature, science limits its goals to proximate truths versus ultimate truth. Science restricts itself, of course, to study of the present, and to those parts of the past for which we have the reliable records of reliable observers.

When science is taken to mean the modern empirical discipline people rightly respect and admire, it is plain that evolution is not science, never was science, never will be science, and never could be science. Science limits itself to the study of observable properties, patterns, and processes in the present; evolution is a belief about the past. The goal of science is to make and to use theories whose predictions can be tested and applied by repeatable observations in nature; evolution is an attempt to reconstruct a unique chronology of singular events that occurred in the past before, supposedly, there were human observers. The purposes of science are pragmatic and restricted to understanding physical phenomena; the purpose of evolution is philosophic, to explain nature and human nature without reference to God (philosophic naturalism) and to make human reason the ultimate court of appeal.

Evolution is not science. Evolution is just humanism dressed up in a lab coat. Evolution itself is a philosophic belief system (naturalism), a complete paradigm or world view, an alternate religion that seeks to explain the origin, history, and meaning of the universe without any reference to a transcendent Creator God. However, evolution likes to dress up in the vocabulary of science, and some deductions from the evolutionist's belief system are scientifically testable. When evolutionary deductions have been tested scientifically, over and over again they have been falsified, proving emphatically that evolution is not science and cannot stand up to scientific criticism. Evolutionists (using anti-Christian lawyers) have resorted to censorship and book banning, trying to protect evolutionary faith from scientific critique in the classroom.

Note well: for Christians, the battle is not between the Bible and science; it is between the Bible and evolution. Science is *not* the enemy of the Christian faith. Indeed, science is the Christian's ally in its battle with evolution!

In spite of initial and increasingly contrary evidence from science, the core belief of evolution has always been and continues to be unflinching belief in long ages of death and struggle. The long ages (with or without God's involvement) are intended to allow time and chance to produce the order that the Bible ascribes only to the Word of God's power — the origin of time, matter, energy, space, stars, planets, and life. Death and struggle is the neo-Darwinist mechanism supposedly operating through so-called geologic time (i.e., fossil deposits) whereby random mutations and natural selection (genetic mistakes and "survival of the fittest") are supposed to transform (with or without God's help) a few simple life forms into the many complex ones we have today. As the late Carl Sagan, the 20th century's most influential evolutionist and humanist summarized it, "the secrets of evolution are death and time."[2]

Belief in long ages of death and struggle contrast sharply with the gospel theme of biblical history: God's perfect creation, ruined by man's sin, destroyed by Noah's flood, restored to new life in Christ. Actually, places for long ages and for death and struggle truly exist in the biblical theme — but not where evolutionists (or Christian compromisers) want them. Unfortunately, death and struggle do fill our world from Adam's sin until Christ's return. Fortunately, long ages are not in the past, out of reach and full of death; the long ages are future and without struggle in the new heavens and new earth when we will have an infinite amount of time to explore an infinite amount of space to learn an infinite amount about our infinite God!

Before we consider interpreting this biblical view in terms of some evolutionary interpretation of science, recall what evolutionists believe about origins:

- **The universe is very old.**

  This premise of an ancient universe is absolutely vital to atheistic naturalism. However, time by itself never made anything happen. Ignoring this, evolutionists trade on the "lottery/casino" mentality that if one tries long enough, good luck is bound to happen. An infinite amount of time, however, would never allow one to roll a 13 on a pair of dice, and the odds against evolution are greater! Besides, as we shall see in later chapters, God has surrounded us with evidence that the earth and universe are young — and His presence is close!

- **The big-bang theory explains the origin of the universe.**

  Not all evolutionary thinkers embrace the big-bang theory, but most do. However, predictions of this theory are precisely falsified by observations of our own solar system, so the evolutionist has retreated beyond science into mathematical speculation wrapped in a cloak of cold dark matter. Claiming to apply Einstein's relativity, they must deliberately ignore the measured effect of gravity on time that Einstein predicted — or accept the evidence of a young universe, fresh from the Creator's hand.

- **Life evolved on earth long ago.**

The famous Miller spark chamber experiment has been used to teach generations of students that nothing supernatural was required for the origin of life — only time, chance, and the properties of matter. Out of necessity, scientists had to abandon that view when they found it was based on the wrong starting materials and wrong conditions and produced the wrong results. A new generation of scientists is finding that the fabulous messages encoded in DNA suggest life is the result of plan, purpose, and special acts of creation.

- **Life developed naturally over millions of years.**

Whether it happened fast or slow, or in a steady or jerky mode, evolutionists insist that a few simple life forms developed into many complex forms by time and chance (random mutations) and struggle and death (natural selection) — what Charles Darwin called "the war of nature, from famine and death."[3] One should understand what the proposed evolutionary process is before hybridizing it with Scripture. Why would anyone want to compromise new life in Christ with millions of years of struggle and death until death wins?

- **The geologic deposits present a fossil record of past ages.**

Darwin knew about the sudden appearance of complex life forms in the lowest fossil-rich layers (what paleontologists now call the "Cambrian explosion" of life). When it came to the intermediate links required to support evolution, Darwin wrote that "Geology assuredly does not reveal any such finely graduated organic chain; and this, perhaps, is the most obvious and serious objection which can be urged against the theory."[4] Could it be that fossil deposits really represent stages in the burial of different environmental zones — the record of a lot of water, not a lot of time?

• ***Ex nihilo* creation is presumed to be a myth.**

Naturalistic theories, by definition and design, exclude the idea of a supernatural, transcendent God. All things that exist must be explained in terms of present processes. Knowledge may change and reveal new concepts, but everything that now exists must have come into existence by forces that were *natural* — not *supernatural* — and hence explainable in terms that include no option of an omnipotent Creator. Darwin's search for a natural explanation was driven by his revulsion at the thought of a God who would allow pain and suffering. His reasoning drove him away from the idea of an omnipotent God, hence the necessity of understanding origins and processes without God. Exclusion of the existence of God is at the heart of all naturalistic and evolutionary thinking. No dogmatic naturalist believes in a Creator. No strict evolutionist accepts *ex nihilo* creative acts.

Over the past 150 years since Darwin, some in the Christian world tried to find ways to theologically accommodate the long ages of death and struggle demanded by atheistic evolutionary thought. This trend of theological accommodation blossomed in the Western world among the more liberal seminaries during the late 1800s and early 1900s. What became known as *theistic evolution* was implicitly assumed in the rise of the so-called higher criticism of biblical interpretation. Over the years, this train of thought was followed by other systems of interpretation, each trying to accommodate evolution in their own way. The following paragraphs contain summaries of the more well-known hybrids.

Theistic Evolution

The early writers of this accommodation to evolution had long embraced the idea that Genesis was allegorical. Because these men believed that Scripture was simply a book of stories, they easily shifted to embrace the so-called science of evolution as the method of God's creation. Genesis had not often been treated literally among the liberal thinkers, so suggesting that God used evolution seemed normal. There really was little attempt to rationalize the differences between the words of Genesis and the teachings of evolution. Scripture was not to be taken literally. God existed, of course, but He was distant and detached, having left His message in the hearts of men only. Now that mankind had arrived at the pinnacle of natural development, the great utopia envisioned by the liberal thinkers could be ushered in.

This theory has waned in popularity among conservative Christians, mainly because those who embraced it in the early part of the last century did not concern themselves with teaching the Bible. Most of the older liberal seminaries are focused now on morals, ethics, politics, history, psychology, and similar areas. Evolution is not questioned. Genesis is irrelevant except as a record of the legends and myths of ancient humanity. These liberal seminaries do not produce books debating the meaning of biblical words, because the words of the Bible are not part of their thinking. A few evangelical seminaries openly espouse theistic evolution, but more have either ignored the issue altogether or embraced one of the other hybrids.

During his hard-fought three-year transformation from evolutionist to creationist, biologist Gary Parker felt the appeal of theistic evolution. Seeing an argument between an evolutionist and a creationist, he liked to step in as a Christian peacemaker, saying, "Calm down. You are both right. Evolution is true *and* the Bible is true. They are just different approaches to knowledge. The Bible tells us *who* created; evolution tells us how He did it."

As he learned more about the God of the Bible, however, Parker felt terrible about trying to give God the credit (blame?!) for evolution. Evolution is based on time and chance; God works by plan and purpose. How could God use chance? How could God use chance on purpose? Those are logical opposites! Even worse, evolutionists believe millions of years of death eliminated the weak and preserved the fittest through the neo-Darwinian struggle for survival. He finally realized that giving God the credit (blame?!) for evolution had several drawbacks:

- It made God the author of struggle and death; yet the Bible says God was grieved to his heart at the violence and corruption that filled the earth after sin (Gen. 6:5–6), and He sent His own Son to heal our suffering and to conquer death.
- Saying God used millions of years of trial-and-error evolution to create makes Him seem more like a bumbling, absent-minded professor than one omniscient, omnipotent Creator. The fossil deposits then become the trash bin where God buried His rejects and mistakes.

Christians who think God could or would use evolution as His means of creation need to re-think both the nature of God and the nature of evolution.

Parker initially thought telling his fellow scientists that evolution was God's means of creation would make it easier to share his embryonic Christian faith with them. He found instead that his colleagues tended to see Christ as just a sentimental fairy tale figure trying to intrude "love conquers all" into the evolutionary reality that "death conquers all."

The Gap Theory

In the 1820s, Thomas Chalmers suggested the idea that a gap existed between an original creation and the present world. He did this mainly to accommodate the long ages espoused by James Hutton and Charles Lyell. Later, the "gap theory" was made especially popular by Dr. C.I. Scofield, who published his teaching notes as an annotated reference Bible in 1909.

Essentially, the gap theory promoted three major points about the early earth. First, Genesis 1:1 described a pre-adamic world, a primal order created during the unknown past. Second, a gap of indeterminate time (long ages) ensued. That world was destroyed by God when Lucifer rebelled and tried to take over heaven. The destruction of that pre-adamic world left the universe "without form and void" as described in Genesis 1:2. (Some describe the long ages of the pre-adamic world as the billions of years of evolutionary development.) The fossils and thick layers of sediments on earth's surface were seen either as the result of God's destruction of the "original creation," condemned when Lucifer rebelled, or of billions of years of naturalistic evolution. Third, the present creation began with the "new beginning" in Genesis 1:3 when God said "Let there be light," and God's "re-creation" work then continued through six literal days.

It was thought by many who embraced this theory that the world of evolutionary geology would be satisfied with this apologetic for the long ages. That did not happen, of course. Common sense and the uniformitarian premises of the geologists rejected the idea that a world, devastated by forces so powerful that the earth would be left "without form and void," could not possibly retain the countless bones of the fossil record. That insoluble problem, and the obvious twisting of the clear text with inserted notes, contributed to the theory's decline.

Gap theorists take the vast majority of Scripture literally, but their exegesis of Genesis 1:1–2 cannot be supported by the hermeneutics that allow them to faithfully understand and apply the rest of Scripture (see Weston Fields, *Unformed and Unfilled*, for details[5]). One particular inconsistency is putting Lucifer's rebellion *before* creation day 6. It is at the end of His creation work that God pronounces everything He created *very good*. Since Lucifer and the other angels are created beings, their rebellion and its effects (which were not at all good) must have occurred after the creation week was complete, not before.

Fossil deposits would, in the young-earth-and-sin view, be related to Noah's flood, which is described in the Bible, and not to "Lucifer's flood," which is nowhere mentioned in Scripture. Gap theorists do want the death and disaster evident in fossil deposits to be Lucifer's fault, not God's. Yet putting fossil deposits before Genesis 1:3 means that God would be calling that worldwide record of death and destruction *very good* — just what the gap theorists do *not* want.

Second, the gap theory grants too much scientific credibility to evolution. Proponents assume evolutionists have strong support for their claims, yet the scientific evidence has been accumulating against evolution ever since Darwin admitted that fossil deposits were the most obvious and serious objection to the theory. Some Christians seem to rush to accept every new evolutionist claim even before the ink is dry on the newspaper. Practical wisdom would suggest that one should know the facts before one tries to find a place for them in the Bible. In cases of apparent conflict, just wait; the scientific study of God's world usually catches up to find that God's Word has been right all along.

Theistic evolutionists see no problem with either science or Scripture, because they accept whatever evolutionists say about science and they do not think Scripture says anything definite at all. Gap theorists generate problems with science and evolution by largely ignoring both.

Credit for maximum misunderstanding of both science and Scripture must be awarded to proponents of the various "day-age" theories.

The Day-Age Theory

The foundational rationale for the day-age hybrid theory, which arose during the 19th century, was the hope that academia in general and scientific education in particular would accept the attempt to harmonize the biblical text with the evolutionary dogma. Once again, the attempt was rejected. No naturalistic evolutionists accept the day-age theory and its supposed biblical correlation with either astronomy or geology. They treated it with even more scorn than young earth creationist thinking, recognizing the inconsistent view of Scripture that the day-age reconstruction required.

As the name suggests, certain proponents of the day-age theory argue that the word "day" not merely *could* but really *should* mean long ages — especially in the context of Genesis 1. Several books and many scholarly articles have been generated to claim that the writer of Genesis meant something different than what he said in the text. Not much was done, however, to deal with either scientific or theological issues — most of the intellectual power and textual criticism was being spent on demonstrating how the days of Genesis could be interwoven with the ages of evolution.

Progressive Creation or Analogical Days

Subsequent to the rise of the day-age theory, serious challenges had begun to surface about the conflict with many passages in the Bible and the theological problems that the kind of God who would use evolution produced. In response to these challenges, some scientifically credentialed Christians began to suggest that the Bible *demanded* long ages (not just "should" mean long ages). These new day-age thinkers insisted that the evidence from what they called science was so overwhelming that the Scriptures had to be clarified by what was "scientifically proven." Although proof is not part of empirical science, the new day-agers assume that science had proven that the universe was billions of years old, that the big bang was an absolute fact, that fossils proved long ages of death and struggle, and, therefore, that one must understand the message in Genesis in the light of science (or, more properly, interpretations of science acceptable to evolutionists).

A few day-age proponents take the position that the days of creation were historical and not allegorical, but they would insist that those days represented scattered periods of God's supernatural activity rather than a sequence of six 24-hour days. The day-age thinkers evolved into analogical creationists. The *analogy* (not allegory) was made with our work week designed by God to set a pattern for life's rhythm of work and rest. Logical connections were more significant than chronological connections, and the initial information in Genesis 1:1–2 was to be understood as background information representing an indeterminate period of time prior to the first "day."

To retain the title of creationists, the leading day-age proponents began to call themselves "progressive creationists," teaching that, while most of the age-long processes were natural processes, God would occasionally create certain vital elements along the way. Most often cited of these elements would be the creation of life from non-life and the creation of man from proto-humans that roamed the earth prior to God's intervention. After having supposedly established itself as a more biblically based and linguistically precise creationist theology than the older ideas of theistic evolution and earlier day-age theories, the main authors tended to heap on the analogy more and more scientific jargon and scientific/historical speculations popular with evolutionists.

The end result of the progressive creationist's combination of naturalistic science with hybrid theology is that the words of scientists supercede the words of Scripture. If progressive creationists were right, we would need a new priesthood of the scientific elite to explain to the rest of us the meaning concealed (not revealed) in God's simple words.

Here are some of the major teachings of progressive creation at odds with a literal reading of Scripture:

- When the words of the text touch areas of interest to scientists, only scientists can tell us what God's word really means.
- Nature is the "67th book of the Bible," and the naturalistic interpretation of nature has authority over the clear meaning of the words of Scripture.
- Eons filled with death existed long before man sinned.
- Death is a natural process that God designed into His good creation.
- A race of soulless *proto-humans* existed prior to Adam.
- God's curse because of Adam's sin involved only spiritual death and not physical death.
- The flood of Genesis was a regional event affecting only Mesopotamia.

Each of these teachings is in direct opposition to the message of Scripture, and taken together they undermine the purpose and work of Christ. Driven by the need to make God's Word compatible with theories popular among evolutionary scientists, progressive creationists refute God's plain words and challenge us to put the words of science experts above the Word of God. Collectively, these teachings attack the biblical definition of the wages of sin and fundamentally assault the biblical view of God and the Christian faith. Insisting that death was a natural process long before Adam attacks the core of Christ's atonement and the biblical teaching of sin's consequences. Later chapters in this book delve into these points more deeply.

The Framework Interpretation

Another revamping of the day-age theory is the framework approach to creation. The Scriptures are evaluated much like any human work of literature. The structure and mechanics of the work are given more weight than its divine inspiration. While trying to maintain that the creation account is historical, proponents of the framework thesis hold that if a portion of the Bible uses poetic or figurative language, then we need not consider it actual history. These teachers arbitrarily conclude that the creation account is figurative and the six days are topical metaphors, which therefore removes the restriction of time.

These interpreters suggest that the creation chapters of Genesis (as well as other passages relating to the creation) are a literary-artistic representation of the creation. Once again, the ideas and words of men are lifted above and against the plain words of God. Nothing so complex is even hinted by the text. The crucial lessons we teach children from the creation account would share authority from lessons we teach from cultural traditions about Santa Claus.

The subtle danger of this approach is its attempt to present itself as conservative exegesis. The main proponents state their affirmation of the historicity of the account, but argue that one of the main reasons Genesis was written was to challenge the polytheism and paganism of early Israel. However, the most discouraging and devastating distortion of framework thinkers (shared by many in the progressive creation camp as well) involves their view of the New Testament sabbath rest (Heb. 4:9–10). God rested on the seventh day from His works of creation, and God is still resting from creative work; therefore — as the interpretation goes — the seventh day is obviously a long indefinite period of time, so the other creation days may be, too. The New Testament "proof" is that the Sabbath rest mentioned in Hebrews is not one literal day. If the seventh day is still continuing, that means sin, death, Noah's flood, and the two-thousand-year war between Satan and the New Testament church all occurred on the age-long day God set aside for rest and worship — given that it is possible to set aside and hallow an unbounded "day" that has not ended yet.

Why would anyone propose exegesis, or even eisegesis, on the basis of such tortuously convoluted logic? Why go through such hermeneutical gymnastics? It is just another attempt (the best disguised so far) to let Christians believe in long ages of struggle and death and still believe the Bible.

Like all the other hybrids, the framework hypothesis starts outside God's Word. Once again, in the name of science, biblical scholars have assumed validity to evolution that is actually contradicted by the scientific evidence at hand. Evolutionists' belief notwithstanding, real science has been unable to find evidence for long ages of death and struggle in God's world; no wonder interpreters cannot find it in God's Word. By providing a theological matrix in which to set the "framework" of creation, the theory takes on the aura of serious biblical scholarship — all the while denying the sequential order and supernatural aspects of the creation.

The Wedge of Intelligent Design

All the hybrid positions described so far uncritically swallow popular evolutionists' interpretation of science, and then use evolutionary interpretations to interpret Scripture. Instead of folding evolutionists' beliefs into the Bible, those involved in the "intelligent design" (I.D.) movement are looking carefully at the science. They have cited numerous examples of biological order that specifically refute evolutionist explanations based on time, chance, struggle, and death and support instead creative processes based in intelligent design.

The motives of the leaders of this I.D. movement seem to be more idealistic and pure than the compromised attempts of previous theorists. While the other "isms" try to make the Bible say something it clearly does not say, the I.D. writers insist that empirical science demonstrates such overwhelming evidence for design that logic alone dictates the necessity for a Designer; and they stick solely to that issue.

By chosen strategy, the I.D. movement makes no attempt to harmonize Scripture and science. Unlike the other hybrid camps, they made the conscious choice to stay away from biblical arguments and concentrate only on scientific data. However (and this is a big *however*), by excluding God from their public discussions and hoping that pure logic will lead others to conclude that God is the Designer behind the design, they have also excluded the power of the gospel (Rom. 1:16). In fact, many of the I.D. group are not Bible-believers of any sort.

By focusing on science, I.D.'s efforts have received less opposition from the scientific community and more acceptance among Christian leaders (because they do not attempt to put the Bible into the equation). Nevertheless, they have not been received by naturalistic evolutionists. True evolutionists have not capitulated to the logic, attributing the design to natural selection. More dangerously, some mystic thinkers have embraced the I.D. concept, trying to milk the wave of Christian acceptance to feed various Christianized brands of "cosmic consciousness."

By avoiding reference to the Bible, I.D. spokesmen are afforded opportunities to reach audiences denied to overtly Christian creationists. Many see their work as pre-evangelistic, and they hope that those whose confidence in evolution has been shaken will look into creationist arguments. Failure to use the

Bible, however, does make I.D. scientists vulnerable to certain evolutionist attacks. When evolutionists "compliment" the Creator for His "responsibility" in creating the AIDS virus and wiping out mistakes like the dinosaurs, I.D spokesmen deny themselves biblical answers based on the Fall and Flood. Unfortunately, even though I.D. evidences erase the need to believe that all order must arise by time, chance, struggle, and death, I.D. leaders refuse to take a stand for the biblical record of creation. They continue to insist on this "neutral" tactic to preserve their accessibility to audiences denied to openly creation scientists.

God cannot be pleased with this neutered approach; for even if one accepts intelligent design, he is still lost in his sins unless he recognizes the Designer as the Creator-Savior of Scripture who died for his sins.

Taking God and the Bible out of the message always leads to human error.

All of These Systems Place Man's Science Over God's Word

The battle between men's words and God's Word has been going on for a very long time. Eve was the first person faced with the choice of taking God's Word literally, or of interpreting it to mean something that was compatible with her own reason and desire. In the first century, Paul warned Timothy to avoid "profane and vain babblings, and oppositions of science falsely so called: which some professing have erred concerning the faith"(1 Tim. 6:20–21).

Evolution certainly qualifies as "science falsely so called." But Paul's words do not refer only to modern experimental science but to all knowledge gained through human endeavor. It is not all human knowledge about which Paul warns us, however, but only that false knowledge built on the false assumption that man's opinion, not God's Word, is the beginning of wisdom.

Why should we avoid that science (knowledge) falsely so called that puts men's words above God's Word? For by professing it, some have erred concerning the faith.

This is not a side issue; it is a salvation issue — rightly understood — as we shall see in the chapters to follow.

It is *not* that one must accept a six-day creation, death after Adam's sin, and a worldwide Flood in order to be saved — *not* at all! But it is true that accepting evolution can be a huge stumbling block to accepting Christ.

Accepting evolution convinces many that man created God in his image, not the other way around, so there simply was no God to inspire Scripture or to keep those wonderful, fairy-tale promises of rich and abundant life after death. Science does not keep people from coming to Christ; science falsely so called, the evolutionary humanists' false interpretation of science that deifies human reason and mutes both God's Word and true science, does. Fitting long ages of struggle and death into the Christian faith does not help. If long ages of death and struggle are true, whether or not God exists, it seems to make God an ogre or, at best, a superfluous hypothesis.

No wonder Paul warned us against science falsely so called. Putting man's earthly wisdom above God's Word, or into God's Word, can be a stumbling block to coming to Christ, and by professing it, some have erred concerning the faith.

The common thread running through these various systems of interpretation is the elevation of men's words above the words of God. The foundation of biblical faith should be — must be — God's omnipotent and omniscient authority. The foundation of atheistic science is naturalistic evolution. The Bible puts man's natural mind in direct juxtaposition and diametric opposition to the Spirit's revelation (1 Cor. 2:14). To insist that the speech of the supernatural creation account declares a naturalistic God is to fly in the face of Scripture (Rom. 1:20). Attacking the foundational message of creation undermines the integrity of Scripture and denigrates the revealed nature of God.

"Thinking God's thoughts after Him," as Johann Kepler noted, is the proper domain of the scientist. Fulfilling the broad stewardship responsibilities implied in the "dominion mandate" (Gen. 1:26–28; 9:1–7) is a wonderful challenge and an exhilarating gift of liberty from the Creator to His regent. Scientists should research and develop. Scientists should probe and explore, wonder and examine, experiment and theorize. Science should "declare the glory of God" (Ps. 19:1). In contrast, when scientists step out of their domain to question the integrity and authority of the Creator's revealed Word, they have usurped their role and entered into the realm of the first rebel. Unscientific speculations about unobserved origins become the basis for a self-serving interpretation contrary to what God's Word says about God's creation. That may be even worse than merely believing a lie.

This issue of biblical authority is not merely one of a favored method of interpretation but rather a frontal assault on the opening declaration of God. Swathed with their science and literary criticism, these theologies become dangerous defamers of who God is and what He has recorded.

> Look unto me, and be ye saved, all the ends of the earth: for I am God, and there is none else (Isa. 45:22).

Table 1: Condensed Definitions of Key Words

Creation — belief that the origin, history, and destiny of the universe, life, and human life is based on God's Word about a perfect six-day creation, ruined by man's sin, destroyed by Noah's flood, and restored to new life in Christ.

Evolution — belief that (with or without God's involvement) the origin, history, and "meaning" of the universe, life, and human life is based on expert human opinion about time, chance, and long ages of death and struggle.

Interpretation — can be correct or incorrect; in the context of this book, it is used in the latter sense: using some extra-biblical concept to suggest a meaning for a scriptural passage different from that conveyed by literal reading.

Literal reading — accepting God's words as if they are intended to clearly communicate, using the rules of grammar, context, and consistency with other scriptural passages.

Science — (1) general: body of knowledge acquired by human investigation; (2) experimental/empirical science: body of knowledge and concepts acquired and tested by repeatable observations of physical phenomena.

Endnotes

1 Charles Colson and Nancy Pearcey, *How Now Shall We Live?* (Wheaton, IL: Tyndale House Publishers, Inc., 1999), p. 32.
2 Carl Sagan, *Cosmos* (New York: Random House, 1980), p. 30.
3 Charles Darwin, *Origin of Species*, text from the 6th ed. 1882 (London: J.M. Dent & Sons Ltd., 1928), p. 463.
4 Ibid., p. 292–293.
5 Weston W. Fields, *Unformed and Unfilled* (Nutley, NJ: Presbyterian and Reformed Publishing Company, 1976).

Chapter 3

Moses and the Prophets

The Gospel of Luke records a particular occasion when Jesus was teaching, as He often did, with messages in parables about the nature of the Kingdom. The crowd was comprised of a mixture of publicans and sinners, His disciples, and some Pharisees. Jesus told those who were hungering, to know of the deep love of their Heavenly Father by picturing God as searching for the lost sheep, the lost coin, and the lost son. Jesus challenged His followers to be wise stewards and "faithful in that which is least" if they were to find the true riches of the Kingdom (Luke 15–16).

Jesus then rebuked the Pharisees because they wanted to justify themselves before men. This, Jesus said, was wrong because "that which is highly esteemed among men is abomination in the sight of God." To illustrate His point, Jesus told the story of a rich man and the beggar, Lazarus. With all of his wealth, education, status, and power, the rich man was sent to hell. Poor, ignorant, filthy, despised Lazarus was carried by the angels to "Abraham's bosom." The rich man, now confronted with the reality of his eternal destiny and the foolishness of his earthly arrogance, begged Abraham to send Lazarus back from the grave to warn his brothers of their impending doom and to reveal the truth to them.

The answer still rings out to us today: "If they hear not Moses and the prophets, neither will they be persuaded, though one rose from the dead" (Luke 16:31).

CHAPTER 4

JOTS AND TITTLES

If one approaches the New Testament account with an open mind and unflinching realism, the evidence clearly indicates that Jesus was an illegitimate child who, when he came to maturity, resented it and was alienated from his parents and siblings.[1]

— Charles Templeton, former evangelist and pastor

The Bible Insists on Supernatural Accuracy

One does not have to be a scholar to know that the Bible contains many passages that declare the trustworthiness of the Bible's words (some have suggested that there are 3,000 obvious references). The consistent message is that God supernaturally influenced the writers of the Bible to such an extent that their words were given divine accuracy (2 Tim. 3:16–17; 2 Pet. 1:21). The message may not be believed, but one can hardly ignore the message permeating the pages of Scripture.[2] It is intriguing to note that the Lord Jesus made a special effort to emphasize the absolute precision of every *jot* and *tittle* of the Law (Matt. 5:18–19). These terms refer to two small pen strokes in the manuscripts. Why such a reference?

Jesus made the *jot* and *tittle* statement in the early part of the famous Sermon on the Mount. Having listed the blessings that would follow those who embrace the message of God and having reminded the listeners that they are to be salt and light in a decaying and dark world, Jesus built the rest of his matchless moral teaching on the eternal nature of the law and the prophets (Matt. 5). His new covenant would not destroy what had been written but would fulfill it. The written records were neither to be done away with nor to be taken as muddy mutterings understood only by the uniquely qualified; instead, they were to be accepted as eternal foundations laid down with precise commandments from the mouth of God. Jesus, the one and only Son of God, had now come to fulfill the promises made so long ago.

"Therefore," Jesus makes careful note to say, "anyone who would break even the least of those commandments would be called the 'least in the kingdom of heaven' "(Matt. 5:19). Anyone desiring God's praise would not want to be called least in His kingdom! What must be His attitude toward Christian scholars of our day who insist on twisting the clear teaching of Scripture to make it mesh with the position of secularists?

The Writings Cannot Be Deconstructed

Jesus was extremely precise in His use of the written words of Scripture. However, some Bible scholars strain to "interpret" biblical words, in spite of the emphasis that Jesus gave to the absolute authority of each word.

After comparing himself to *the* door that opened to eternal life and *the* Good Shepherd that would give His life for the sheep, Jesus publicly declared that He and His Father were one (John 10:30). The religious scholars of the day immediately reached for stones to execute Him on the spot and denounced Him for His "blasphemy." Jesus' calm response was to quote from Psalm 82:6. Note that Jesus called Psalm 82 "law" and insisted that the writings could not be broken. Jesus, using very strong terminology in His message in John 10:35, said that there is absolutely no way possible (no power, no ability) for the writings to be dissolved (melted, loosened, broken apart).

This song of Asaph is a difficult passage, yet it is easy to understand the application that Jesus made by citing the reference as proof of His claim to equality with the Father in heaven. The word *Elohim* is a well-known term used throughout God's Word. *Elohim* was the Creator (Gen. 1:1). *Elohim* brought the destruction of the first age (Gen. 6:13). *Elohim* talked with Abram and promised to establish His covenant (Gen. 17:7). *Elohim* called to Moses out of the burning bush (Exod. 3:4–6). No Jew alive would have ever mistaken the powerful comparison that Jesus cited in Psalm 82:6. The word *Elohim* had centuries of history and meaning behind it. The word meant exactly what it meant.

No one — certainly no Jew — would have given an instant's thought to another meaning. They knew what Jesus was claiming; they just refused to accept it. They wanted to kill Jesus for claiming to be God. Never had a debate existed about the meaning of the word *Elohim*. The people simply rejected the words of Scripture in favor of their own interpretation. In this case, the religious leaders had their own theology. That theology did not allow for a humble, common man who talked about seeking the lost and forgiving their sins to claim equality with *Elohim*, no matter how many miracles He worked!

Some of today's Bible scholars excel in attempting to break the Scripture! Volumes are written in an effort to interpret the words of God in ways other than the way intended by God. A form of logic, scholarship, and appeals to science are used to deconstruct the language. Pains are taken to convolute the grammar, rewrite the history, superimpose the culture, twist the nuances, invent connotations, cite reams of references, and so forth — all with a conscious intent to change the clear meaning of the words of God.

Jesus not only emphasizes the precision of the words and the ideas and concepts they convey — He does not give any room to wiggle. The written Word is the anchor. Those who want to play with the words of Scripture (the writings) must do so in defiance of that which the Lord Jesus said is the law that cannot be broken (John 10:35). Sadly, many Christian leaders in today's churches break that law and try to make wiggle-room when there is none.

Every Word of Scripture Is Precisely the Right Word

Jesus corrected a poor interpretation of His messianic role by demanding that the Pharisees recognize a clear use of two different terms (in the *poetry of the Psalms*) that dealt with the rule of the Messiah (Matt. 22:41–45). Several points are important to observe in this use of Scripture. Jesus specifically said that David was "in spirit" when he penned Psalm 110 and that *Yahweh* (the LORD) said to David's *Adonai* (owner, master) that He (the *Adonai*) was to sit at the right hand of *Yahweh* until His enemies were conquered. "How then," Jesus asks, "can the *Adonai* be David's son?"

Jesus proves His deity on the basis of specific *written* words.

The text is absolutely precise. Not only are the different terms exact, but the careful use of the personal and possessive pronouns allows for only one interpretation. The proof Jesus cites is in the modifiers *the* and *my* and the fact that *Lord* is a different word in both cases. In the first case, the definite article *the* precisely pins down the specific God of heaven; in the second case, David precisely limits his relationship to "that" LORD by making it clear that *the* LORD is *my Adonai*. The language does not allow for David to be the father of *Yahweh* or the king of David's *Adonai*. Evidently, every word is critical to a right understanding of the passage. Jesus does not permit a different interpretation! The words mean exactly what the words say, and the specific words give a precise meaning to the teaching.

It seems inconsistent as well as irreverent for those who claim to believe in inspiration and inerrancy to imply that the Holy Spirit is a sloppy writer. Some in different religious camps, of course, do not believe in any kind of supernatural authority or accuracy for the writings of the Bible. They are at least consistent with their insistence that the Bible must be "interpreted" in the light of scientific and/or "more accurate" information. It is contradictory for those who claim to believe in a God who cannot lie — a God who has revealed His Word to us, a God who wants us to know His will — to insist that we *must* interpret the Bible to fit human science or intellect. Doing so treads on very dangerous ground.

Even the Tenses Are Absolute

Earlier in Matthew 22, Jesus referenced God's declaration to Moses at the burning bush (Exod. 3) to refute the Sadducees' revisionist thinking about the Resurrection. The Sadducees brought up the hypothetical case of a woman who had had seven husbands. This, in their enlightened thinking, would show how foolish the idea of a bodily resurrection was. But Jesus bluntly stated that they had made two errors: one, they did not know the Scriptures, and two, they did not know the power of God (Matt. 22:29). Then He quoted from Exodus 3:6, stressing the tense of the verb *to be*, to remind them that "God *is* not the God of the dead, but of the living" (Matt. 22:32, author's emphasis).

Two points must be understood: Jesus uses "the writings" — the written words — and says that they are "spoken unto you by God" (Matt. 22:31). There is no doubt about His teaching. There is no alternate interpretation. There is no other meaning. The words mean what they mean. They were spoken to us by the God who does not lie. They were written down so we could not make a mistake. Also, those spoken writings are so accurate that even their tenses hold eternal truth!

Clearly, Jesus insists that the written words are *the* words God caused to be recorded and that their meaning, their grammatical use, and even their tense is eternally correct and supernaturally accurate. Jesus, by His own use of the words of the Scriptures, teaches that every word is exactly the word that God wanted to use in any given passage.

We are faced with opposite alternatives: Jesus is either an ignorant religious zealot — or worse yet, a conscious liar — or He is the Creator God, explaining to us how carefully He caused His word to be communicated. It is not possible to have it both ways. Any attempt to harmonize these conflicting ideas is foolish. Those who deny the deity of Jesus Christ reject the idea of biblical inspiration outright. They are consistent in their belief and in their logic. Sadly, some Christian scholars claim to believe in inerrancy and inspiration yet attempt to "interpret" the written words of God to fit the ideas of the atheist, naturalist, or evolutionist. *That* is illogical.

God Does Not Hide His Revealed Words

If the words of the Bible can be "interpreted" to mean whatever we want them to mean, then the words are meaningless! It simply does not make sense. If God hides His revelation so that only the "scholars" can understand it, then God is both a respecter of persons and deceitful. If it is necessary for every man or woman to know the linguistic nuance and cultural setting of a given word before it can be "properly" understood, then God is being deliberately misleading when He says things like:

- The secret things belong unto the Lord our God: but those things which are revealed belong unto us and to our children for ever, that we may do all the words of this law (Deut. 29:29).
- As for God, his way is perfect: the word of the Lord is tried: he is a buckler to all those that trust in him (Ps. 18:30).
- All scripture is given by inspiration of God, and is profitable for doctrine, for reproof, for correction, for instruction in righteousness: That the man of God may be perfect, throughly furnished unto all good works (2 Tim. 3:16–17).
- Knowing this first, that no prophecy of the scripture is of any private interpretation. For the prophecy came not in old time by the will of man: but holy men of God spake as they were moved by the Holy Ghost (2 Pet. 1:20–21).
- Blessed is he that readeth, and they that hear the words of this prophecy, and keep those things which are written therein: for the time is at hand (Rev. 1:3).

That brings up the questions: Why would anyone even want to "interpret" what God says? Why would anyone want to make the words say anything other than what they say? Why would some want to make "day" mean "billions of years"? Why would anyone want to blend the evolutionary theology of long ages of death and struggle with new life in Christ? Could there be an ulterior motive?

Men Change the Word of God Because They Do Not Like What It Says!

The only answer to the questions above is that those who change the meaning do so because they do not like what the words say. Jesus drew the same conclusion.

> But he answered and said unto them, Why do ye also transgress the commandment of God by your tradition? For God commanded, saying, Honour thy father and mother: and, He that curseth father or mother, let him die the death. But ye say, Whosoever shall say to his father or his mother, It is a gift, by whatsoever thou mightest be profited by me; And honour not his father or his mother, he shall be free. Thus have ye made the commandment of God of none effect by your tradition.
>
> Ye hypocrites, well did Esaias prophesy of you, saying, This people draweth nigh unto me with their mouth, and honoureth me with their lips; but their heart is far from me. But in vain they do worship me, teaching for doctrines the commandments of men (Matt. 15:3–9).

Jesus also noted that Isaiah said what he said because:

> For laying aside the commandment of God, ye hold the tradition of men, as the washing of pots and cups: and many other such like things ye do. And he said unto them, Full well ye reject the commandment of God, that ye may keep your own tradition (Mark 7:8–9).

Jesus exposed the cultural and religious tradition that the Jewish spiritual leaders were using to undermine, nullify, and reject the words of God. He called them hypocrites. They were more interested in building a case for their interpretations than in keeping the commandments of God. What must His attitude be toward those who foster interpretations that teach long ages of death before sin as though it were biblical truth?

The Logic and Philosophy of the World Robs Us of Truth

The apostle Paul warned the sophisticated church in Colosse, immersed in their Greek intellectual training and culture, that they could be cheated (the word has a strong, negative connotation — *rob, spoil, plunder*) by philosophical arguments and the broad principles of man's worldly logic. "Beware lest any man spoil you through philosophy and vain deceit, after the tradition of men, after the rudiments of the world, and not after Christ" (Col. 2:8). This warning comes after a specific set of instructions. We are to use the riches of full assurance of understanding; acknowledge the triune godhead in whom are hid all the treasures of wisdom and knowledge; watch out lest we should be beguiled with enticing words; maintain order and a steadfast faith in Christ; continue to walk in the same way we received Christ; be rooted and built up in Christ, being established in the faith as we have been taught; and abound in that teaching with thanksgiving (Col. 2:1–7).

Not much room for permission to manipulate biblical data exists in those verses!

Our Christianized Western culture has become centered on questioning what the Bible "really" says. We have shifted from submitting to the authority of the words of Scripture to musing about the thoughts of Scripture. We have moved off the pages of the written text to the "dynamic translation" or the "literary framework" to speculate on what God might mean. More dangerous than this is our exaltation of academia to the point that a scholar or a leader is measured by how many books he has written or read — books that have been accepted by the widest audience. The measure of these books is not whether they meet the criteria of the written word of God, but whether they are lauded by the broadest spectrum of men!

May God forgive us and change us. We have allowed an attitude to creep into the training of our best and brightest so that they love "the praise of men more than the praise of God" (John 12:43).

The Bible Demands Obedience to God

The Bible is unique among all books. Not only is it different in its form, structure, and history, but it also takes the position of supernatural superiority to all other communication. It insists on total accuracy for its content and on absolute obedience to its commands. No other book is so demanding.

Two hundred fifty direct commands in the books of the Old Testament and over 50 in the New Testament demand obedience to the instructions of God. One may not believe the requirements, but one cannot argue that these statements are not presented in every section of Scripture. Even elementary human logic would conclude that such instructions would have to be clear if they are to be obeyed. How can a person obey a command which cannot be understood? How could a God who insists on obedience blur His instructions with words that do not mean what they say? What kind of God would purposefully obscure His instructions?

Because the Bible so obviously insists that Jesus Christ is the only way to God (John 14:6), thousands of the world's greatest scholars, kings, priests, and philosophers — acting independently and in concert over centuries — have endeavored to disprove its claims, expose its teachings, or destroy its pages. All have failed. The Bible has proven to be more historically and archaeologically accurate than any other ancient book. It has been subjected to the minutest scientific and textual analysis possible and has been proven to be genuinely authentic in every way. The followers of the Bible's teachings have been persecuted and martyred and have had their copies of the Bible burned or mutilated, only to have the believers multiply and flourish in an unprecedented way. The history of the Bible is truly remarkable.

Although much in the Bible is testable in terms of history, science, and archeology, it is primarily a revealed message from our Creator that spans all cultures, backgrounds, languages, and times. That message is this: God, the everlasting omnipotent, omniscient, omnipresent, transcendent Creator of the universe, designed and created two beings to bear His image and have eternal fellowship with Him. These beings were charged with stewardship dominion over the earth and told to fill the earth with their children. That first human pair, created in perfection and in harmony with all that the Creator designed, dared to rebel against the Creator's authority and embrace another "truth." The consequence of that rebellion is that humankind — including you and me — are born into this universe as sinners under God's condemnation. That is a frightening set of beginning parameters! Yet, they are not given without hope. The Old Testament describes the awful plight of the condemned sinner and promises the eventual coming of a Redeemer who will buy back the rebel from the enslavement and condemnation of sin. God loves His created beings, in spite of their rebellion, and has done the only thing possible to provide the means of satisfying His righteous judgment and rescuing us from an eternity of condemnation. The New Testament illustrates the beautiful fulfillment of the Old Testament promises in the presentation of God's only begotten Son, Jesus, the Christ.

God's Written Word Is God's Supernatural Record

Much evidence supports the claims of the Bible. However, the central message cannot be tested in a laboratory by scientific analysis or verified by archaeological research. The foundation of truth begins in Genesis, where we learn about the unique creation of man and man's rebellion and fall from a perfect relationship with his Creator. If this initial and foundational record is not true, if the words of that record are only an allegory or a framework from which we may meander limitlessly through our imagination, if we may "interpret" the words any way we believe to suit the scholarship of the moment, then *we* become the storytellers!

It is important to remember that God, through different messengers in different venues over time, gave His message by the written word. The God who wrote this message repeatedly states in Scripture that He caused His words to be supernaturally communicated from Him and by Him to us, so that we who so desperately need to know the truth could have revealed to us what is true! His words are to be accepted as evidence and substance of God's veracity. That is what the Bible calls faith. We are told that "without faith it is impossible to please [God]" (Heb. 11:6). From a biblical perspective, our faith (and therefore all of our relationships with God) starts, continues, and ends with our belief in the words of God. Any way one wants to evaluate that assertion, the words — the written words — are the focus of our faith.

It has been said that trying to understand the words of the Bible is not important; instead, what is important is having Jesus in one's heart. Really? How can one know it is Jesus who is in the heart, and not a false christ? Is a warm, fuzzy feeling to be our evidence? Hinduism and Mormonism can provide warm, fuzzy feelings. Are good deeds the measure? Many atheists excel at good deeds. Could it be the rules one obeys? A Muslim may obey more rules in one day than a Christian does in a month. We need the words of Jesus to know Jesus the Word. Otherwise any false christ or personal preference fills the hearts and guides the faith. The Bible's message does not allow for any mixture or compromise.

One of two positions must follow: either the Bible is what it claims to be — the written revelation of truth from God the Creator — and as such is to be trusted, studied, and obeyed; or, the Bible is a meaningless collection of myths and legends, that, although interesting and full of curious things, represents only the evolutionary record of primitive man trying to cope with the unknown.

> So then faith cometh by hearing, and hearing by the word of God (Rom. 10:17).

Endnotes

1 Charles Templeton, *Farewell to God* (Toronto: McClelland & Stewart Inc., 1996), p. 93.

2 Examples of biblical references on verbal inspiration:

- The Ten Commandments were audibly delivered in such a way that the assembled nation of Israel heard the instructions. God then wrote them on stone tablets with His own finger (Exod. 20:1; 31:18).

- Moses insisted that none of the words of the Commandments were to be changed by adding to or taking from them in any way (Deut. 4:2; 12:32).
- David knew that the words he was writing were inspired by the Spirit of God (2 Sam. 23:2).
- Jeremiah had a keen awareness of God's word in his heart (Jer. 20:9) and heard God speak directly to him (Jer. 30:1). Also, he was told to speak and precisely record exactly what he heard (Jer. 26:2; 30:2; 36:2).
- Isaiah received a supernatural visit from God (Isa. 6:1–8) and knew that God was directly in control of the message that he was preaching (Isa. 59:21).
- The poet (Ps. 12:6) as well as others (Prov. 30:5–6) insisted that God's words were to be taken as absolutely pure.
- Jesus claimed to say only what God the Father instructed (John 12:46–50) and that the words of God are eternal (Matt. 24:35).
- Paul knew he was given supernatural revelation (Rom. 16:25–26; 1 Cor. 11:23; Eph. 3:3) and confirmed that his writings were God's commands (1 Cor. 14:37; 1 Thess. 2:13; 2 Thess. 2:15).
- Jesus insists on the accuracy and the authority of the written words of Scripture (John 5:39; Luke 24:25, 27, 44; Matt. 5:17–18), citing both the creation account (Matt. 19:4) and the Jonah account (Matt. 12:39–40) as actual history.

Chapter 5

According to Your Faith

I think a case can be made that faith is one of the world's great evils, comparable to the smallpox virus but harder to eradicate.[1]

— Richard Dawkins

In a rather dramatic climax to his search for the Holy Grail, Indiana Jones (Harrison Ford) steps off into nothingness to prove his faith. The eighties Hollywood production *Indiana Jones and the Last Crusade* was built around a search for the mythological artifact which was supposed to be the cup from which Jesus drank at the Last Supper. Indiana Jones and his dad (Sean Connery) follow a series of clues gleaned from painstaking archeological research. The last and final clue was a "leap of faith" which would lead them to the Holy Grail.[2]

On many a long road did they wind, fraught with perils real and imagined, but at last they arrived at the long-hidden site (interestingly enough the magnificent tombs of Petra), only to be confronted by a horrific fight with the villains. The elder Dr. Jones is shot and lies dying on the floor of the cave; Indiana Jones is called on to save both his dad and the day.

Carefully he works his way through the perils of the treacherous inner cave, only to find himself teetering precariously on the edge of a bottomless chasm. There is no way to cross. The "salvation" of his dad lies across the abyss, the arch fiend is taunting in the background, and the situation looks hopeless. Suddenly, Jones clutches at "the book" in his bosom. "It's a leap of faith," he proclaims. To which his dad responds, "You must believe, boy. You must believe." With grim determination written on every pore of his face, Indiana places a hand over his heart, arches his leg out over the gulf, and steps out into thin air.

Of course, the hero does not fall. A "miraculous" bridge crosses the gap, hidden in plain sight by an optical illusion. Indiana Jones identifies the Grail and rescues his father. What is the lesson conveyed? "Believe" hard enough and the right things will happen — even when reasonable and responsible people would think you are nuts! What a wonderful example of faith!

No, it is not!

Faith Is Defined Precisely in the Bible

Hebrews 11:1 contains the most clear-cut definition of faith recorded in Scripture. It is imperative that those who would claim to have a personal relationship with Jesus Christ (who is "the author and finisher of our faith," Heb. 12:2) understand this simple and defining statement: "Now faith is the substance of things hoped for, the evidence of things not seen" (Heb. 11:1). The word translated *substance* in the King James Version of the Bible is a Greek word that simply means *substantial nature, essence, or reality*. Faith is the essence or reality of our *hope*. The word translated *evidence* is the translator's choice for a Greek word that is also an uncomplicated term meaning *proof*. Faith is the *proof* of things "not seen." Faith looks forward based on a present evaluation of *things* that we do not yet have and cannot now see.

Whenever and however *faith* is expressed, it demonstrates these two basic characteristics: it *believes* in things not yet received but assuredly expected, and it *believes* in things that cannot be seen through human intelligence or experience. Christian faith is taking God at His word and acting accordingly.[3]

Faith Is Critical to Our Relationship with God

Some very interesting events took place when Jesus was on the way to the house of a nobleman named Jairus. Recorded in Matthew and Mark (Matt. 9:18–26; Mark 5:22–43), these passages help us understand the importance of God's words in the matter of our faith.

Jairus had begged Jesus to heal his little daughter who was terribly sick and at the point of death. "I pray thee, come and lay thy hands on her, that she may be healed," he had said. So Jesus, who always responded to the needs of the hurting, started to walk toward Jairus' home, followed by a crowd of the curious. In the crowd was a woman who had been very sick for 12 years. She had spent a lot of money on treatments and advice from various physicians, but was not getting better. In fact, she was getting worse. She had no doubt heard about the healer from Nazareth and was so confident that He had more power than the physicians that she thought to herself, *If I may touch but His clothes, I shall be whole.*

Faith "Believes" in the Reputation of Jesus Christ

We are not given any other background on this sick woman. We do not know if she had seen any other miracles performed by Jesus or if she had seen Jesus *do* anything. We do not know when or where she had gained her faith. For all we know, the only information she had acquired prior to her personal contact with Jesus in the crowd was testimony from others about what Jesus was preaching. Maybe all she had had was a faithful teacher who had shared with her the promise of the coming Messiah. What we *do* know, however, is that her faith was so important to the success of her healing that Jesus said, "Thy faith hath made thee whole . . . and be whole of thy plague."

Her faith? Faith in what? Certainly not in doctors! Obviously, not in herself. Clearly, the object of her faith was the person of Jesus — or more precisely in His *reputation*! The lady believed what she had been told about this Jesus, this healer of the sick and this One who had power to cure when no doctor could.

What is there about the reputation of the Lord Jesus that is so powerful? Ponder that thought while we continue to walk with Jesus to the nobleman's house.

Jairus must be excited and encouraged. He has just seen a very sick lady healed of her incurable disease and heard the Lord

Jesus honor that lady for her faith. He had faith. He had acted on that faith. Jesus *could* do what He said! His daughter *was* going to be healed! While Jesus was still speaking, one of the servants from Jairus' house pushed his way into the inner circle of the crowd and blurted out to everyone that Jairus was not to trouble the Master anymore. The girl was dead.

Talk about throwing cold water on a growing flame! You can hear the hiss and crackle of sputtering faith as Jairus tries to absorb the attack on his faith in Jesus. Just as his faith had received a wonderful lift from seeing the power of God in action, Jairus' trust was challenged with the scientific fact that his daughter is dead, dead in every way that the "modern" science of the day could gauge death. Everybody at Jairus's house, and most of the crowd as well, thought that this was the end of the matter. "She's dead," they all told Jairus. "Don't trouble the Master anymore." One can imagine the crowd thinking, *God can't bring the dead back to life. God has to be limited by His own physical laws. The girl is dead, for crying out loud!* Words that bring doubt have terrible power.

The Bible says faith comes by hearing the Word of God (Rom. 10:17). The gospel of salvation is the "power of God" (Rom. 1:16). Words that undermine the words of God throw against faith a counter force, a force that seeks to crush belief with doubt. No matter how they come — whether from a servant of the house, a professor with a list of degrees as long as your arm, or a Bible-thumping preacher from the pulpit — if the words are counter to the Word of God, they will damage faith in God.

Faith Believes When Experience Is Contrary to God's Word

The people in the house only saw the dead body of the little 12 year old, and they *knew* that nothing could be done. Their faith was in what they saw. Their belief was in what was physically (scientifically) evident. They did not believe in miracles; and, even when Jesus, the Creator of life, spoke to them directly, they *still* did not believe! They laughed and mocked and made fun of this preacher who told them that death could be overcome by the authority of God. It is certain that the majority of those participating in this moment in history based their belief on the "evidence" — the dead body.

Jesus must have known what a terrific blow the news of his daughter's death was to Jairus. However, this was the moment when God was going to display His supernatural power. "Be not afraid," Jesus said to Jairus, "only believe." Only believe? Believe what?

The crowd would have Jairus believe that his daughter was beyond the help of God because the laws of science were unbreakable. Jairus's servant would have him believe the servant's tender, carefully planned, empathetic announcement of her death. Was Jairus to believe the obvious "evidence" that everybody else believed? Should he believe that Jesus could heal the sick but not raise the dead? Should he rethink, reevaluate, and reconstruct what had happened to fit the evidence of the moment?

Fortunately, Jairus believed that our supernatural God could overrule the natural laws He created. Unlike Eve, Jairus "believed" God's Word over man's word. Even though the news of the death of his daughter hurt him deeply, his faith was in the God of heaven and earth, the One who had *created* life! Jairus believed that all Jesus had to do was "lay His hand" on his daughter — dead or alive — and she would be made whole. Jairus's faith was in what *God* said, not what man could prove. He believed; he trusted; he had confidence that God was right.

Faith Believes in Spite of What the Crowd Says

A similar event occurred as Jesus exited Jairus's house. Two blind men, sitting in the street close to the house, found out from the crowd that Jesus was nearby. They began to shout for Jesus to "have mercy" on them and followed Him down the street for some distance, insisting on His intervention. There was no medical cure for their blindness. No human experience or logic could give them any hope. Yet, they were confident in the supernatural authority and power of God. When Jesus finally gave them His attention, He asked them if they "believed" that He could heal them. Interestingly, Jesus then simply said, "According to your faith be it unto you" (Matt. 9:29). Their faith would make them whole.

In a similar incident several months later, two other blind men (one named Bartimaeus) were sitting on the road outside the city of Jericho (Matt. 20:29–34; Mark 10:46–52; Luke 18:35–43). When these men heard that Jesus was passing by, they began shouting for Him to "have mercy" on them. (No doubt the event at Jairus's house had been fairly well publicized.) The crowd rebuked the blind men for making such a scene, but Bartimaeus shouted all the louder, "Jesus, thou son of David, have mercy on me!" (Mark 10:47).

Jesus stopped in the road and insisted that the shouter be brought to Him. Bartimaeus threw off his beggar's cloak and moved forward, groping toward the voice. Jesus asked, "What do you want me to do for you?" Jesus was not searching for diagnostic information. Bartimaeus was blind! He needed to see. Jesus wanted Bartimaeus to confirm what he needed and to trust the One who made man's eyes to heal him. Once Bartimaeus verbalized his need, Jesus stated again, "Thy faith hath saved thee" (Luke 18:42).

According to their faith, it happened. Is that the measure by which God judges us or works in our lives? Does the level (amount, quality, depth, firmness) of our faith affect the way God reveals himself to us?

Faith Is Based on the Word of God

It is absolutely clear from the written words of Scripture that our faith in God is based on hearing the Word of God.

> The word is nigh thee, even in thy mouth, and in thy heart: that is, the word of faith, which we preach; That if thou shalt confess with thy mouth the Lord Jesus, and shalt believe in thine heart that God hath raised him from the dead, thou shalt be saved. For with the heart man believeth unto righteousness; and with the mouth confession is made unto salvation. For the

> scripture saith, Whosoever believeth on him shall not be ashamed.
>
> For there is no difference between the Jew and the Greek: for the same Lord over all is rich unto all that call upon him. For whosoever shall call upon the name of the Lord shall be saved. How then shall they call on him in whom they have not believed? and how shall they believe in him of whom they have not heard? and how shall they hear without a preacher? And how shall they preach, except they be sent? as it is written, How beautiful are the feet of them that preach the gospel of peace, and bring glad tidings of good things! But they have not all obeyed the gospel. For Esaias saith, Lord, who hath believed our report? So then faith cometh by hearing, and hearing by the word of God (Rom. 10:8–17).

What seems to be unusual is the targeted undermining of God's words by many compromisers who claim to be biblically conservative or staunchly evangelical and insist that they believe in the inerrancy of the Bible. Why would anyone who claims to submit to the authority of God's Word question the words of God? How can someone who has placed his faith in the person of Jesus Christ argue with what He said He did in any part of His Word? What kind of logic would demand inerrancy on the one hand and support deconstruction of the language of Scripture on the other?

When can one depend on the text, and when can one question? Who is qualified to decide? Who dares to change the meaning of a word that God caused to be written?

Faith Does Not Let Science Supersede God's Word

It is amazing how much of the evangelical world believes science or expert opinion over and above, or perhaps more correctly stated *instead of*, the Bible. It should not come as a shock that the crowd, walking through the wide gate, refuses to believe the words of God. The majority has never followed God

(Matt. 7:14). Even the religious elite of Jesus' day (both "left" and "right") believed their scholars and their traditions more than the written Word of God. What is disappointing, however, is when those who claim to be disciples of Jesus make a conscious effort to force His words to say something they do not.

Never, never confuse biblically based science with atheistically driven science.

Science, both biblical and empirical, is based on observable and demonstrable knowledge. *Knowledge* — that is the key word. Observation of our world provides a vast amount of information and data from which we draw knowledge. Two Bible passages describe this legitimate search for knowledge:

- And moreover, because the preacher was wise, he still taught the people knowledge; yea, he gave good heed, and sought out, and set in order many proverbs (Eccles. 12:9).
- Whom shall he teach knowledge? and whom shall he make to understand doctrine? them that are weaned from the milk, and drawn from the breasts. For precept must be upon precept, precept upon precept; line upon line, line upon line; here a little, and there a little (Isa. 28:9–10).

The process of knowledge acquisition is as follows: pay attention (observe); seek answers (test, experiment, and verify); and document the results. The process is limited by the level of maturity (knowledge, skills, and understanding) of the seeker, and by the diligence of building concepts on clear and unchanging precepts. These precepts are colored and strengthened by the supporting data, but those are not found in one place or at one time. That process and those criteria are both biblically and scientifically sound.

Science involves discovering information and predicting effects that can be tested. It is then necessary to reproduce the test or to document the test procedures so that others can achieve the same results when they perform the test. Finally, it is important to continue to evaluate the test results; we may achieve a level of knowledge which will reveal faults in our premises and force a change in our thinking. In short, to be considered science or scientific, a piece of knowledge must be testable, reproducible, and falsifiable.

It is interesting to note that even the United States Supreme Court acknowledged the above criteria in the 1993 *Daubert* v. *Merrell Dow Pharmaceuticals* case.[4] In the decision, the Supreme Court set aside a broad "general acceptance" test that had been the standard since1923. Although the ruling specifically applied only to scientific evidence presented in federal court under Rule 702, the essence of the ruling was precisely in line with the biblical criteria. One wonders why we are so particular in a court of law but not in "regular" science or theology.

We have fairly extensive knowledge of *what* things are and an ever-growing understanding of *how* things work. We step outside the realm of scientific knowledge, however, when we attempt to construct a scenario describing *when* or *how* things that do not happen now came into being at some time in the unobserved past.

The scientific method has yielded an enormous amount of knowledge. Science is truly a remarkable discipline, in both its pure and applied forms. After data are uncovered, research typically produces a useful product or process. Because products and processes that come from the scientific method improve our lives in one way or another, we are tempted to look at science as the ultimate and complete basis for understanding the world. Most of the time, science is beneficial, aiding mankind in having biblical dominion over the earth.

We get ourselves into deep trouble, however, when we attempt to apply scientific methodology to fields of knowledge that cannot be validated by such means. Important fields beyond the reach of scientific method include philosophy, ethics, politics, history, and origins. When it comes to origins, we get into particular trouble when we attempt to transform *assumptions* about processes or events into facts.

Faith is SUPERnatural and Outside Testable Science

The fiercest attack on Scripture today is against three foundational elements of the Bible: (1) the historicity of the creation week, (2) the fall of man and the subsequent introduction of God's sentence on His creation, and (3) the horrific destruction of that first world by the worldwide flood in the time of Noah. Scientists who are committed to naturalism refuse to believe any of these accounts.

Indeed, naturalistic science should *not* and cannot deal with the first two of those events, or with the extremes of the third. Why not?

Science has no testable way to verify — or refute — the origins events recorded in the Bible. They were unique and unrepeatable. We can study the results of past origins events and how things function now, but nothing today is being created. God maintains His creation by regular, repeating processes scientists call natural law, the normal domain of science. How does this apply to origins? Science can only verify what it observes and tests, so origins are outside the scientists' reach. Those scientists who reject the words of God can only state opinions and rework data to come up with naturalistic scenarios for what is only explainable by supernatural causes. Imagine the difficulties scientists would face if they were forced to explain the origin of an airplane on the basis of time, chance, and physical processes, ruling out ahead of time the evidence of plan, purpose, and acts of engineering. If one does not accept the precepts of Scripture, one must reason without the insight of the only observer of those events. Unlike the evolutionist who is limited only to human observations, the creationist has both human and divine observation, plus an accurate historical record!

Despite the advantages of scriptural knowledge, even the Apostles had trouble believing events beyond their natural experience.

They were with Jesus in a small fishing boat crossing over the Sea of Galilee when a sudden wind arose. Jesus was tired from His earlier ministry and was asleep in the back of the boat, resting on a pillow. The Apostles let Him sleep for a while (they really did love Him) while they tried desperately to manage the boat in the growing storm. It soon became obvious that the wind and the waves were way beyond their ability to handle, and the boat began to fill with water (Matt. 8:23–27; Mark 4:35–41; Luke 8:22–25).

"Master," they shouted as they ran over to awaken Him, "we are dying! Don't you care?" Then came the famous words: "Peace, be still." The wind and the waves immediately calmed.

The Apostles were stunned. They probably stared at the water and at each other for a few moments with looks of incredulity. This could not happen! Wind and waves do not obey someone's command. What kind of man is this? In their desperation they begged Jesus to save them; but when He did, they could not believe it.

They could not believe it? All of them had been traveling with Jesus for some time. While they had been together, they had seen Jesus miraculously heal a leper, speak to a Roman centurion about his great faith when his son was healed, and cast out a demon. Most of them were present earlier when Jesus told them where to catch a multitude of fishes and were in the room when Peter's mother-in-law had been healed of a terrible fever. Why then could they not believe it when Jesus calmed the storm? They had plenty of examples of the power of God residing in the Christ.

It is no wonder that Jesus said, "O ye of little faith" (Matt. 8:26).

What was Jesus implying in that statement — that the Apostles had a small amount of faith? Is there a difference in the kinds of faith? Just what is Jesus dealing with here? Perhaps the answer to these questions comes from the section of the Bible that defines faith.

Faith Has Its Foundation in Creation

Immediately following the Bible's own definition of faith comes the Bible's prime example of faith — the creation:

> Through faith we understand that the worlds were framed by the word of God, so that things which are seen were not made of things which do appear (Heb. 11:3).

Genesis 1 and 2 are written so clearly and are so easy to read that the creation account is identified as the first and primary foundation for our faith. The things that God made are the signature of His godhead, written in infinite but soundless speech that can be understood by all.

> The heavens declare the glory of God; and the firmament sheweth his handywork. Day unto day uttereth speech, and night unto night sheweth knowledge. There is no speech nor language, where their voice is not heard (Ps. 19:1–3).

In fact, the language is so clear that God will execute His wrath on any creature that dares to change the language into an "image" that mars His glory and majesty.

> Because that which may be known of God is manifest in them; for God hath showed it unto them. For the invisible things of him from the creation of the world are clearly seen, being understood by the things that are made, even his eternal power and Godhead; so that they are without excuse: Because that, when they knew God, they glorified him not as God, neither were thankful; but became vain in their imaginations, and their foolish heart was darkened. Professing themselves to be wise, they became fools, And changed the glory of the uncorruptible God into an image made like to corruptible man, and to birds, and fourfooted beasts, and creeping things (Rom. 1:19–23).

How many of us understand the real importance of the creation? Just look at the effort that is being exerted by the enemies of God to disprove supernatural creation and to embrace some form of evolutionary and naturalistic (read "atheistic") explanation for what we see in our telescopes and microscopes. What we may be missing is how fundamental the message of the creation is to the whole of Scripture. One can believe in God (the devils do — James 2:19) and still not exercise the kind of faith that saves (Eph. 2:8). Maybe God's work of creation is more important than we think. *Maybe* it is not possible to find faith if we ignore the universal language of creation.

Faith Believes in the Supernatural Power and Authority of God

Hebrews 11, considered the "Faith Chapter," contains what some call "Faith's Hall of Fame." This record concentrates on the subject of faith and lists a series of heroes that exemplified a life of faith. All of these persons acclaimed by God believed in the supernatural power and authority of God. *All* accepted challenges or endured horrific tortures rather than deny or ignore God's power and authority in their lives. Just what does the Scripture conclude about these wonderful people? They "obtained a good report through faith" (Heb. 11:39). These incredible lives, these monumental heroes in the eyes of our Creator God, all lived and accomplished their eternal testimony through *faith!*

Their faith was a faith —

- based on the assurance and conviction that God is the Creator;
- based on the hope and unseen fact that God exists and that He rewards those who "diligently seek Him" (Heb. 11:6);
- that saw the eternal power of the godhead in the things that are made, and understood that the worlds were made from things that do not appear (Heb. 11:3);
- that heard the preached word and believed with the heart;
- that did not listen to "enticing words of man's wisdom," but rested in the "power of God" (1 Cor. 2:4–5).

Hybrid theologies, which attempt to blend the atheistic assumptions of evolutionary naturalism with the transcendent omnipotence of the Bible's Creator, undermine the core foundation of our faith. If the Bible is not trustworthy in its opening sentence, what about the rest? Upon what basis do we select certain portions to believe by faith while rejecting others? If we truly believe that God has either been unclear or has not told us the truth about His work in creation, then how can we trust Him with our eternal destiny? It is no accident that the creation account is a continual battlefield for our faith.

According to your faith be it unto you (Matt. 9:29).

Endnotes

1 Richard Dawkins, "Is Science a Religion?" *The Humanist*, 57 (January/February 1997): 26.
2 Steven Spielberg, director, *Indiana Jones and the Last Crusade*, VHS, (Hollywood: Paramount Studio, 1989).
3 Defining faith biblically:
- Faith is not subject to a scientific method (Heb. 6:17–19).
- Faith is not subject to man's test (Eph. 2:8–10).
- Faith does not base its hope in present conditions (Rom. 8:24–25).
- Faith is not dependent on human explanations or understanding (Isa. 55:8–11).
- Faith is, however, both reasonable and defendable (1 Pet. 3:15).

4 *Daubert* v. *Merrell Dow Pharmaceuticals, Inc.*, 509 U. S. 579 (1993).

Chapter 6

Written with the Finger of God

As a story of creation, the Book of Genesis long, long ago crumbled under the weight of science, notably Darwin's theory of natural selection.[1]

— Time

Why Was the Creation Personally Emphasized by God?

For the scientifically sophisticated citizen of the 21st century, what is the most embarrassing verse in the Bible? Is it a verse about supernatural bodily resurrection? That *was* the reason for rejecting or re-interpreting God's Word for the scientifically savvy in the 1800s, but not today. Today "everyone" who believes in reincarnation accepts "resurrection," so apparently wishful thinking still trumps science. For those wanting to be thought scientific today, the most embarrassing verse may be Exodus 20:11, "For in six days the Lord made heaven and earth, the sea, and all that in them is."

Try this experiment sometime. Walk into a shopping mall, tap someone on the shoulder, and then say, "Hi. I believe God created people and the whole universe in six days a few thousand years ago." Will they laugh at you? Almost every time. (Unfortunately, the experiment produces the same result in too many churches, Christian colleges, and seminaries.)

Those who stood up for Jesus Christ and the authority of God's Word in the 1st century were crucified upside-down, burned at the stake, boiled in oil, and tossed to the lions. What happened to the Christian church? It grew and prospered and conquered the Roman Empire!

What happens to Christians who stand up for Jesus Christ and the authority of God's Word in the 21st century? People laugh at them. What do Christians do? Many just melt. (Most of us can remember a time when we would rather be dead than be laughed at.) It is a very effective technique.

If laughter and ridicule are such effective techniques, why did God not warn us about them? He did. In 2 Peter 3, God warns us about the scoffers coming in the last days. Those scoffers are interested in neither the facts of God's world nor God's Word. "They willingly are ignorant of" the records of both God's acts of creation and God's judgment on mankind's sin at the Flood (2 Pet. 3:5). By their scoffing ignorance, however, they cheat themselves out of a place in a "new heavens and a new earth" (2 Pet. 3: 7, 13).

All Scripture is inspired by God, but the Ten Commandments were inscribed by God (Exod. 24:12 and 31:18)! The fourth commandment, written with the finger of God, includes God's personal summary of His own creative work:

> For in six days, the Lord made heaven and earth, the sea, and all that in them is, and rested the seventh day: wherefore the Lord blessed the sabbath day, and hallowed it (Exod. 20:11).

Jesus, whom the apostle John identifies as the Creator (John 1:1–3) certainly accepted the historicity of the creation account (Matt. 19:4–5), and referred to it in His earthly ministry. Around heaven's throne, Jesus will be forever honored as the Creator:

> Thou are worthy, O Lord, to receive glory and honour and power: for thou hast created all things, and for thy pleasure they are and were created (Rev. 4:11).

From the very beginning, the creation account and God's work as Creator is central to God's message to mankind — from the beginning of time all the way through to the glorious consummation of history (His story) in eternity.

Unique to Genesis, in comparison to all other "religious" writings, is its opening line: "In the beginning God created the heaven and the earth" (Gen. 1:1). In every other religious book, the event of creation is not directly discussed or is described in a way that is anthropomorphic (man-centered) and evolutionary. The Bible is the only religious book that cites a specific beginning and that declares that an eternal, omnipotent, omniscient, transcendent, and personal God created the entire universe. Oh, there are gods aplenty in ancient writings and creative acts described in various stories. These sources talk about bringing order out of chaos. But those gods, either barely intelligent titans or lustful and capricious beings that can hardly be trusted, are VERY different from the God of the Bible.

This radical distinctive of the biblical beginning is repeated and emphasized in the uplifting and soul-satisfying words of the other Bible book that begins "In the beginning. . . ."

> In the beginning was the Word, and the Word was with God, and the Word was God. The same was in the beginning with God. All things were made by him; and without him was not any thing made that was made (John 1:1-3).

This "Word" is revealed as none other than the incarnate Son of God, Jesus the Christ:

> And the Word was made flesh, and dwelt among us, (and we beheld his glory, the glory as of the only begotten of the Father,) full of grace and truth (John 1:14).

How incredible! The transcendent Creator of the universe, the author of life, the One who made mankind in His image steps out of eternity and into time and space to give rest to the weary (Matt. 11:28), to bring back the wandering, and to seek and to save the lost (Luke 19:10). Gone is the back-breaking burden of pagan religions with their paths one must climb to reach God; instead, it is God in Christ who reaches down to seek us.

Pale and pathetic by comparison are the evolutionary cosmogonies that arrogantly assert, as if it were science, that matter produced mind, and that impersonal forces produced personality. No! It was mind which came first — the mind of God, the wisdom of God, the Word of God — and His mind created matter by the Word of God's power! Nor was it impersonal forces acting by chance through which personality emerged from the ooze of our ancestry. No! Personality came first, in the three persons of the triune God; and it was their love — neither evolutionary need nor necessity — that brought other persons into being.

Why would anyone who trusts in the gospel of John 3:16 want to compromise the biblical beginnings in Genesis 1:1 and John 1:1 with the "science falsely so called" of evolutionary cosmogony, chemical evolution, or evolutionary anthropology?

It is obvious, of course, that evolutionists must reject the supernatural, purposeful beginning described in the Bible. The blinders of philosophic naturalism restrict their search for truth to the realm of naturalistic, purposeless processes. Evolutionists must begin with matter, not mind, and with particles, not personality. Astronomer Harlow Shapley expressed the evolutionist's far-deeper-than-science presupposition in these ringing words, "In the beginning was the Word, it has been piously recorded, and I might venture that modern astrophysics suggests that the Word was hydrogen gas."[2]

Shapley's most famous student, the late Carl Sagan, once was responding to questions from the audience on a television talk show. When asked where the hydrogen (i.e., the first matter) came from, Sagan insisted that the question be answered with another question: "Where did God come from?"[3] Actually, that really is the correct question. Something has to have always been here. Either matter is eternal, or God is eternal.

Scientists have measured that every time matter changes form, it loses some useful energy, order, or information. Any two or all three of these may be lost. It is contrary to a vast body of repeatable, observable, testable scientific measurements to claim that matter (mass energy) is eternal. Eternal matter makes no sense; eternal God does.

Yet in spite of the real science, some Christian leaders want to hybridize the biblical teaching "In the beginning God" with the naturalistic "In the beginning was hydrogen." Some try to insert long ages, if not death and struggle, into the biblical narrative by suggesting that God created the earth out of old material.

"In the Beginning" Means in the Beginning

"In the beginning . . ." (Gen. 1:1). Every time that phrase is used in the rest of Scripture, it *always* means "in the beginning!" — at the start, before something else happens, originally, at first, initially, and at the outset. Every one of the 17 times that phrase is used — whether it is referring to the creation or the harvest or the reign of a king or the New Testament gospel — it means the same thing. Why would we want to make that phrase mean anything else? Even when scholars attempt to analyze the Old Testament word for beginning, *re'shiyth*, and its close Hebrew synonym, they are both describing the start or the head of something. Most of the time the Hebrew word *re'shiyth* simply means "the beginning." In every case, the rest of the sentence (context) clarifies how the words are to be understood.

Why should it be any different with the first verse of Scripture? Why should "beginning" not mean "beginning"? Why is it that so many scholars want to deconstruct the words and replace the normal, clear, precise, easily understood meaning with another long-winded explanation of how "nature" and "science" have proven that God really did not mean what He said?

In the beginning, there was a *start*. Time itself, it seems, was God's first creation. Why would anyone want to suggest otherwise? The answer to that question lies in what one chooses to believe, not in the linguistics.

"Create" Means Create!

In the beginning, at that start, God created. The Bible nowhere hints that God tried out various random acts of nature on pre-existing matter for eons of unmeasured time. All of the language used, indeed the very choice of the words used, makes it clear that God created something where nothing existed before.

- "And God said . . . " (Gen. 1:3, 6, 9, 11, 14, 20, 24, 26).
- By the word of the LORD were the heavens made; and all the host of them by the breath of his mouth (Ps. 33:6).
- For he spake, and it was done; he commanded, and it stood fast (Ps. 33:9).
- Let them praise the name of the LORD: for he commanded, and they were created (Ps. 148:5).
- I have made the earth, and created man upon it: I, even my hands, have stretched out the heavens, and all their host have I commanded (Isa. 45:12).
- And, Thou, Lord, in the beginning hast laid the foundation of the earth; and the heavens are the works of thine hands (Heb. 1:10).
- For God, who commanded the light to shine out of darkness, hath shined in our hearts, to give the light of the knowledge of the glory of God in the face of Jesus Christ (2 Cor. 4:6).

The Scriptures are certainly consistent. God, being who He is, has told us that He created all things. By the revelation of himself in the things that He has created and by His own statements in His Word, we know that creation was initiated out of God's own will and pleasure — using designs, energies, and actions that only He could perform. There was nothing but himself from which things came. There was no space: He stretched it out. There was no time: He began the beginning. There was no matter: He spoke and it was so.

Even the Hebrew word, *ba-ra'*, is absolutely precise. The Holy Spirit of God chose this word to use in the profound message of the first set of written words communicated from God to man. It is used in 46 verses of the Old Testament and is consistently translated just like it is rendered and used in the first verse of the Bible. In the few places where the translators chose another English word rather than "create," it is clear from the context that the passage is using the word figuratively to speak about a new condition that is going to come about as a result of some unusual action.

If God had wanted to state that He allowed natural processes to create the world, He could have conveyed His meaning more clearly by the use of several other Hebrew words. The Hebrew *caphiyach,* for instance, used in Job 14:19 and other places, describes things that grow of themselves. This would have been a good word to use if the Lord had wanted to describe inherent mechanics in creation that would encourage self-development. The word *qarah*, which means "to happen" (chiefly by accident), is another good word that God could have used if He had wanted to convey that creation happened over time.

However, God did not use those other words: He used *ba-ra'*. That word always means "to create; to make something happen that is new and fresh and unique." *Ba-ra'* describes what only God can do with His unique power. *Ba-ra'* requires power that man does not have — power to create *ex nihilo* (out of nothing). The biblical account is very specific. Everything was *created.* "Things" did not evolve slowly out of natural forces that were acting on eternally existing matter. The words and the sentence structure of the recorded creation account could not be clearer: in no passage anywhere is there a hint of a time of unknown ages. All of the data — all of the record in this historical narrative — is structured in such a way that we cannot conclude that long ages are involved — unless, we go to great lengths to explain away what is clearly written.

Once again, one has to ask the question: if God uses *ba-ra'* and not *aphiyach* or *qarah* or any other Hebrew word to speak about creating, then why would anyone want to change the obvious meaning of the word He did use to one He did not use?

Here is an ironic twist. Boldly emblazoned on the cover of the April 2002 issue of evolution-touting *Discover* magazine are these eye-catching and sadly amusing words:

> **Where Did Everything Come From?**
> The universe burst into **something**
> from absolutely **nothing** — zero, nada
> And as it got bigger, it became filled with
> even more stuff that came from absolutely
> **nowhere**. How is that possible?
> Ask Alan Guth. This theory of inflation helps
> **explain everything.** (emphasis in original)[4]

For years those who would hybridize Scripture with evolution said the biblical doctrine of *ba-ra'* creation from nothing (*ex nihilo*) is a scientific embarrassment. Now "science" (or at least Alan Guth) is saying that "the universe burst into **something** from absolutely **nothing**," and that "helps **explain everything.**" Since the mathematical magic of a sophisticated scientist has made it intellectually chic to believe nothing explains everything, perhaps the compromisers will grudgingly allow the creationists to take *ba-ra'* literally, as in creation *ex nihilo*.

There is, however, a difference. Guth believes that before everything there was absolutely nothing. According to the Bible, before everything in the universe there was the transcendent, supernatural God far above and beyond and before and after the universe. He created (*ba-ra'*) the universe without using (*ex nihilo*) pre-existent time, matter, energy, or space. Everything did *not* come from "absolutely nothing"; it came from I AM — the omnipotent, eternally existent Word of God!

Maria's line in *The Sound of Music* still eloquently summarizes the discoveries of science: "Nothing comes from nothing;

nothing ever could." Apart from God, mass-energy can be neither created nor destroyed. That concept, and Maria's song, should point us beyond nature and naturalism to the one true God.

Day Means "Day"

The word, "day" (*yowm*), appears to be the most embarrassing word in the Bible, or so it would seem. Debates in the church past have swirled around words like justification, sanctification, predestination, and even Resurrection. Now, in this advanced scientific age, many theologians struggle with the word "day" and pass their confusion and uncertainty through the seminaries and Christian colleges into the churches and onto the people in the pews.

The famous attorney Charles Darrow called attorney William Jennings Bryan to the witness stand in the famous "Scopes Monkey Trial" (there was a perverted caricature of that trial in the Hollywood film, *Inherit the Wind*). To show the world's press the utter foolishness of trying to take the Bible in an intellectually serious fashion, Darrow asked Bryan two simple questions: (1) Where did Cain get his wife? and (2) Were the days of creation ordinary days? Despite his well-deserved reputation as an eloquent Christian spokesman, Bryan ducked one issue by saying he was not concerned with other men's wives and the other by claiming that he was willing to allow days to be long ages. As a result of that public humiliation, compromise positions blossomed. Biblical authority retreated from American life. In this round, "science" won; "religion" lost.

Because of such compromise, some Christians now teach that it "enlarges" our view of God to believe He shaped the human body through millions of years of refinement. Later, the teaching continues, God finally gave spiritual life to hominoids which enabled them to separate sufficiently from other primates. It is scientifically embarrassing, these teachers would assert, to claim that God molded the dirt of the ground directly into an adult male who could talk and name animals. How, then, would such teachers account for Lazarus? Before Jesus finished the three words "Lazarus, come forth!" He turned a liquefying, decomposing mass of flesh into a full-grown, walking, talking human being. If the living Jesus did not literally do that for Lazarus, how can we trust the crucified Christ to raise our corrupted corpses "in the twinkling of an eye"?

Even more important than the time issue, however, is our willingness (or not) to take God at His Word. If we tell our children that they cannot really accept the clear and simple words with which God begins His revelation, will they really want to try to guess what the hard words might mean? How would we know anyway? How powerful will be our witnessing and missionary efforts if we must clarify the meaning of confusing and culturally dependent words like "day."

As used in Scripture the term is quite understandable. *Yowm* is used hundreds of times in the Old Testament. Sometimes the word is translated "time," as in "many days." Sometimes it is used in a way that implies an indeterminate amount of time — as in "day of trouble" or the "day of the Lord." In the majority of cases, however, the word is used just as we would use it: to designate a specific day of the week, a certain day of the month, a special day, or a celebration or sequence of days. The usage is always ordinary and easily understood. It is not a vague term.

Now the key question: is the meaning of "day" clear in Genesis 1? Is it the ordinary period of time like that we experience today? Do the scriptural words, grammar, and context let God tell us what He means by "day" in Genesis 1? The answer is an emphatic yes!

In the creation account (Gen. 1:1–2:4), God linguistically defined the term "day" with a specific and precisely limited meaning. In every passage in the Bible where creation days are mentioned, the use of "day" is absolutely consistent with the very carefully defined application and meaning in Genesis 1. By this very specific word, God is ensuring that we understand His message.

After He had separated the light from the darkness, God called the light "day" *(yowm)*. The darkness, God called "night" (Gen. 1:5). Again, using the term in the ordinary way we still use today, God uses "day" both for the day/night cycle and for the lighted portion of each cycle. As though God wanted to further emphasize what He had in mind when He used the term "day," He said "the evening and the morning" (the dusk and the daybreak) "were the first day." God repeated that precise formula for every one of the six days during which He constructed the universe! Everywhere else in Scripture that "day" is used with a number, with evening and morning, or with evening or morning, it always means an ordinary day. To make sure we cannot legitimately miss His meaning, God piles emphasis upon emphasis.

God made *light* on day one, then on day four, God made *lights (ma-or)* to rule over the day and the night (Gen. 1:14–18). These "light bearers" were to provide a time reference to guide all of the creation — to divide the day from the night. They were to be "for signs, and for seasons, and for days, and years." God set up a clock system to be sure that we would always understand time. The basis of that clock — the day — marks dusk and daybreak with the precision and familiarity of the tick of a second hand.

It is hard to conceive of a more precise way to define "day" with words. The first three days were not "solar days" since the sun had not yet been created. But that does not *mean* the first three days were a different length than those following. An hour measured by a sun dial is not different in length, from one measured by an hourglass or an atomic clock. Only the measuring device changed, not the length or the day God had already established as His fundamental unit of time.

God's first creation "in the beginning" was time. It is not surprising that He established a unit for us to use to mark the flow of time; that unit is one familiar day. On day four, God puts that familiar unit in the context of other familiar time units, seasons and years. (If days are not days what would seasons and years be?!)

If words mean anything, the days of the creation week are the same length as those we experience today. Had God wanted to be indefinite about the amount of time involved in creation, He certainly could have been. In Genesis 2 God recounts creation in terms of mankind's relationship to it, and the time involved is not highlighted. In Genesis 1, however, God stresses His emphasis on time, telling us emphatically to relate His creation days to our ordinary days.

When God issued the fourth commandment, He specifically wrote, in clear letters carved in stone with His own finger, that we were to remember the sabbath day and make it holy because:

> For in six days the Lord made heaven and earth, the sea, and all that in them is, and rested the seventh day: wherefore the Lord blessed the sabbath day, and hallowed it (Exod. 20:11).

Disconnecting the fourth commandment from the creation week takes some serious hermeneutical gymnastics! To suggest that this God-given reason for the "rest day" is somehow connected to long ages, one must redefine the entire meaning of the context as well as rewrite the dictionary. Rather, by the obvious comparison in Exodus 20:11, it appears that God went out of His way to connect an ordinary 24-hour day/night cycle with the creation week.

In fact, when Jesus was defending His behavior on the day of rest (the sabbath) to the legalistic and hypocritical Pharisees, He told them that they had misunderstood why God hallowed the sabbath in the first place.

> And he said unto them, The sabbath was made for man, and not man for the sabbath: Therefore the Son of man is Lord also of the sabbath (Mark 2:27–28).

Notice the point God made. He designed the creation *week* so that man could rest. Jesus made the days of the week for man. Therefore, He (Jesus) is Lord (Owner, Master, Creator) of the sabbath. No reason exists for redefining the word "day" to mean "ages" — unless another agenda must be met.

There are Bible teachers and professing Christians with scientific training who try to incorporate long ages into the creation days to make Genesis 1 more acceptable to "science," or more accurately, the evolutionist's interpretation of science. If one were to ask an honest scientist (one not imprisoned by philosophic naturalism): "How long did it take for earth to form?" Such a scientist might well reply:

> As a scientist, I have no way of knowing. Science limits itself to the study of processes repeatedly and objectively observable in the present. If I assume some process always occurred in the past at the rate observed today, I could estimate a maximum age — but my answer would be no better than my assumption. Besides, the same assumption for different processes yields radically different results. Furthermore, I have evidence in the present that suggests many process rates were different in the past. If you really want to know how long it took to form the earth, you really need to find an historical record from a truly reliable observer.

What resource does the Christian have? The absolutely reliable record of the ultimately reliable observer and Creator, the Lord God, maker of heaven and earth! When we ask our loving Heavenly Father, and listen with trusting faith, He tells us in plain language that can be understood by all people at all times in all places, that "in six days the Lord made heaven and earth, the sea, and all that in them is." The answer to how long it took is "six days" — six days like those in our work week. That simple, yet profound and powerful message, was even written with God's own finger in a tablet of stone!

Consider this, too. If God used a term that clearly means one thing in the ordinary, everyday sense, but redefined this term to mean something else, then it appears that God is hiding rather than revealing the truth. If the terms God used are wrong, if the terms convey a lie, if God is purposely misleading us — we have a real problem.

The age issue is the most visceral of all the debates between creation and evolution. Even more serious concerns will be addressed in later chapters, but among Christians, the meaning of the word "day" is at the core of the age debate. If the earth is young, then the evolutionary and naturalistic approach to science is abruptly blocked since an evolutionary scheme of development *requires* long ages to function. The Bible text does not appear in any way to support such a long-age idea — especially with the use of the term "day":

- God defines the term "day" with great precision in Genesis.
- God's first use of the word describes the daylight portion of a day/night cycle.
- God equates the days of creation with work-week days in the fourth commandment.
- God inscribed the fourth commandment with His own finger.
- God specifically insists that the "rest day" was made for man.
- God modified the word "day" with numerals (i.e., six days) and ordinals (i.e., first day) and modified it with evening and morning.
- God verifies the historicity of Genesis through the Lord Jesus.

The terms describing the creation week are not vague. The normal and natural reading of the text (Hebrew or English) would never lead one to "believe" in evolutionary eons nor would it render any meaning other than a 24-hour, ordinary day.

One of the more prominent Hebrew scholars of the 20th century was Dr. James Barr, professor of Hebrew at Vanderbilt University and former regius professor of Hebrew at Oxford University. Below is a comment he made in 1984, in a letter to David Watson:

> Probably, so far as I know, there is no professor of Hebrew or Old Testament at any world-class univer-

> sity who does not believe that the writer(s) of Genesis 1–11 intended to convey to their readers the ideas that (a) creation took place in a series of six days which were the same as the days of 24 hours we now experience (b) the figures contained in the Genesis genealogies provided by simple addition a chronology from the beginning of the world up to later stages in the biblical story (c) Noah's flood was understood to be worldwide and extinguish all human and animal life except for those in the ark. Or, to put it negatively, the apologetic arguments which suppose the "days" of creation to be long eras of time, the figures of years not to be chronological, and the flood to be a merely local Mesopotamian flood, are not taken seriously by any such professors, as far as I know.[5]

Dr. Barr may have missed a professor or two, others may have come along in the ensuing decades who embraced this Orwellian-type "doublethink" regarding the text of Genesis. However, all the books and public debates espousing long ages in Genesis that have been written by Christian scholars insist that Genesis means something other than what it states. Dr. Barr's point is that no evolutionist takes seriously the compromise arguments of those Christians who create eons out of days.

The language of Genesis is not confusing. The words are clear; the message is clear; and the meaning of the words is clear. Some folks just simply do not want to believe what the words say!

Why Do So Many Object to God's Written Words?

When we clear away all the high-sounding reasoning, the real issue seems to be the authority of God's Word.

Some speak of "dynamic equivalence," by which they appear to mean that the more authoritative message comes from the thoughts behind the words. Many popular modern Bible versions are products of this dynamic equivalence school of thought — they fall somewhere between a verbatim translation and a paraphrase. Of course, unless one is a knowledgeable student of the manuscripts, it is not easy to tell where translation ends and "dynamics" begin.

Others subject the words of Scripture to scholarly criticism by using a "literary framework," which cites the poetic style of the Hebrew language as support for their non-historical view of the creation account. Once again, human scholarship is the filter through which we are supposedly enabled to understand the "real meaning" of God's message. Besides, although the language of Genesis 1 is majestic, it does not bear the marks of Hebrew poetry. The first Hebrew poetry is Adam's response to the creation of Eve (which ladies are welcome to find most flattering).

Proponents of "open theism" insist that God imposes limits on himself in order to deal with human creatures. Because, the argument goes, He desires people to be free in their responses (man's free will), God cannot know what a given individual response will be. Therefore, God changes His mind or His plans based on His reactions to what people actually do. Although a debate still prevails regarding this view, a growing number of widely known and highly influential people (among non-literalists) are raising a ruckus about those who resist their "openness" to question the authority of God's Word.

Please do not miss what is happening in the scholarly world. The argument is not about "inspiration" or "inerrancy." That argument seems to be over — in the sense that far more scholars reject verbal inspiration than accept it. No, the argument is over "academic freedom" to explore new avenues of thinking — new ideas that will give intellectual status to thinking that distorts and demeans the words of the Bible. Even in conservative Christian circles, much of the debate seems to be one scholar's defense or criticism of another scholar — one argument vying against another to become the "top" rationale with more logic and scholarship than other arguments. Why does the human mind tweak or interpret or (in some cases) defy the words of God?

The language of creation is so clear and so important (Ps. 19). Is it any wonder that we are warned of dire consequences if we do not listen to the One who now speaks (Heb. 2:1–4) —

especially when we have received knowledge of the truth (Heb. 10:26–27) and this truth concerns God's creation (Rom. 1:18–20)? The Bible says, "All scripture is given by inspiration of God . . ." (2 Tim. 3:16). Once we question the inspiration of God's words, we subjugate the obvious meaning of the words to someone or some thing other than God. The Bible says that "every word of God is pure" (Prov. 30:5). Yet once we qualify the purity of the words, we have set ourselves up as the arbiter of the message. Once we interpret Scripture according to our personal preferences or personal beliefs, we have violated God's principles.

What about the millions of non-scholars? How do ordinary people find faith? Did the millions who lived and died prior to the modern "enlightenment" live in ignorance? Do only a few in each generation get to understand God's Word correctly? Is God's word hopelessly sunk in the quagmire of "deep" scholarship? Is it possible for "ordinary" people to understand what God has recorded?

Surely, God did not write His Word only for the educated!

Remember the lessons of the Bereans (Acts 17). Because God's Word is written for the common man, the Bereans could check out the expert (the apostle Paul, no less!) as they "searched the Scriptures daily, [to see] whether those things were so" (Acts 17:11). Remember also the lesson for the experts: communicate God's Word plainly, pointing hearers to God's wisdom and not yours.

What is needed from experts is not more scholarship but more humility before the living Word of the living God. Addressing controversy over the word "day" in his time, Martin Luther stated it this way:

> But if you cannot understand how this [the creation] could have been done in six days, then grant the Holy Spirit the honor of being more learned than you are.[6]

Why Did God Create Anyway?

One of the most often overlooked factors about God creating is the "why" factor. Why did He do what He did? Why did

He speak things into existence? Why did He demonstrate His omnipotence and omniscience so magnificently and clearly?

- *Creating expressed the direct will of God.*
  Thou art worthy, O Lord, to receive glory and honour and power: for thou hast created all things, and for thy pleasure they are and were created (Rev. 4:11).

- *Creating gave God a universal language.*
  The heavens declare the glory of God; and the firmament sheweth his handywork. Day unto day uttereth speech, and night unto night sheweth knowledge. There is no speech nor language, where their voice is not heard (Ps. 19:1–3).

- *Creating eliminated excuses for all humanity in all circumstances.*
  For the invisible things of him from the creation of the world are clearly seen, being understood by the things that are made, even his eternal power and Godhead; so that they are without excuse (Rom. 1:20).

- *Creating gave foundation to the everlasting gospel.*
  And I saw another angel fly in the midst of heaven, having the everlasting gospel to preach unto them that dwell on the earth, and to every nation, and kindred, and tongue, and people, Saying with a loud voice, Fear God, and give glory to him; for the hour of his judgment is come: and worship him that made heaven, and earth, and the sea, and the fountains of waters (Rev. 14:6–7).

- *Creating displayed the power of the Lord Jesus Christ.*
  For by him were all things created, that are in heaven, and that are in earth, visible and invisible, whether they be thrones, or dominions, or principalities, or powers: all things were created by him, and for him: And he is before all things, and by him all things consist. And he is the head of the body, the church:

who is the beginning, the firstborn from the dead; that in all things he might have the preeminence (Col. 1:16–18).

- *Creating gave authority to the message of Jesus Christ.* God, who at sundry times and in divers manners spake in time past unto the fathers by the prophets, Hath in these last days spoken unto us by his Son, whom he hath appointed heir of all things, by whom also he made the worlds; Who being the brightness of his glory, and the express image of his person, and upholding all things by the word of his power, when he had by himself purged our sins, sat down on the right hand of the Majesty on high (Heb. 1:1–3).

- *Creating established Jesus Christ as the source of life.* In the beginning was the Word, and the Word was with God, and the Word was God. The same was in the beginning with God. All things were made by him; and without him was not any thing made that was made. In him was life; and the life was the light of men.

  He came unto his own, and his own received him not. But as many as received him, to them gave he power to become the sons of God, even to them that believe on his name: Which were born, not of blood, nor of the will of the flesh, nor of the will of man, but of God. And the Word was made flesh, and dwelt among us, (and we beheld his glory, the glory as of the only begotten of the Father,) full of grace and truth (John 1:1–4, 11–14).

- *Creating is what God does when He gives new life.* For by grace are ye saved through faith; and that not of yourselves: it is the gift of God: Not of works, lest any man should boast. For we are his workmanship, created in Christ Jesus unto good works, which God hath before ordained that we should walk in them (Eph. 2:8–10).

Creating is what God does! Creating is what *only* God can do! Creation is way beyond the understanding of human intellect and experience. That is precisely why God caused the record of His relationship with man and requirements for man to begin with an exact account of His omnipotent and omniscient work.

Is it credible to assume that God would carefully design His own purpose and character into the very creation itself and insure that the record of that originating event be precisely transmitted — emphasizing the activity in the writing of His own finger — only to abandon those records to the variegated whims of those who place their own opinions on a higher plane than His Word? Logic cannot support an inspiration that is protected by man or an inerrancy that is preserved through man. If one says that he believes in the God-breathed accuracy of Scripture, then he should at least take the God-written words at face value!

The words of the LORD are pure words (Ps. 12:6)

Endnotes

1 Robert Wright, "Science and Original Sin: Evolutionary Biology Punctured the Notion of a Six-day Creation, but Biblical Themes of Good and Evil Are More Robust," *Time*, October 28, 1996, p. 76.

2 Preston Cloud, editor, *Adventures in Earth History*, "On the Evolution of Atoms, Stars and Galaxies," by Harlow Shapley (San Francisco, CA: W. H. Freeman and Co., 1970), p. 78–79.

3 Michael Colombo, "Nothing but Faith in Nothing," quoting Carl Sagan, TruthinCinema, http://www.truthinstuff.com/Cinema/contact.html (accessed September 26, 2003).

4 Brad Lemley, "Guth's Grand Guess," *Discover*, April 2002, front cover text.

5 James Barr to David C.C. Watson, April 23, 1984.

6 Ewald M. Plass, compiler, *What Luther Says: An Anthology*, Vol. 3 (St. Louis, MO: Concordia Publishing House, 1959), quoting Martin Luther, p. 1523.

CHAPTER 7

GOD SAW THAT IT WAS GOOD

What kind of God can one infer from the sort of phenomena epitomized by the species on Darwin's Galapagos Islands? The evolutionary process is rife with happenstance, contingency, incredible waste, death, pain and horror.[1]

— David Hull

The position that long ages of death and struggle are part of God's creation work is dramatically contrary to the meaning of the word "day" in Genesis 1, as defined and clearly delimited by God himself. Far more contrary than putting long ages into the creation week, however, is putting death and struggle into the creation period about which God himself calls everything *very good* (Gen. 1:31). Making death and struggle part of God's perfect work of creation is contrary to the nature of God, contrary to the Word of God, contrary to God's revelation of himself in His world, and the exact opposite of the whole wonderful message of redemption in the gospel of Jesus Christ.

A major term repeated almost as often as "day" in Genesis 1 is the word "good." At the end of each of the creation days (except the second), God calls what He has done "good." At the end of the creation week, He pronounces all His creative work *very good.* The question arises, why did God make these comments? Why was it necessary to qualify His work? What was there about His work that required a comparative observation to be made? Furthermore, against what is the *good* to be measured? Why not simply provide an objective, *just-the-facts* report? Why this unusual emphasis?

Perhaps the answers lie in the observations themselves.

What Is "Good"?

The definition of the Hebrew word that God chose to use in Genesis 1 to describe His satisfaction with the work accomplished is not all that complex:

> *Towb*: good (as an adjective) in the widest sense; used likewise as a noun, both in the masculine and the feminine, the singular and the plural (good, a good or good thing, a good man or woman; the good, goods or good things, good men or women), also as an adverb (well): beautiful, best, better, bountiful, cheerful, at ease, fair (word), (be in) favour, fine, glad, good (deed, -lier, -liest, -ly, -ness, -s), graciously, joyful, kindly, kindness, liketh (best), loving, merry, most pleasant, pleaseth, pleasure, precious, prosperity, ready, sweet, wealth, welfare, (be) well ([-favored]) (Strongs 2896).

The above definition is taken from the *Strong's Exhaustive Concordance*, which also lists the various English words that have been chosen to represent the occurrence of *towb* in the Old Testament. *Towb* is a common word, a simple word. It always speaks of something that is good, nice, pretty, or pleasant. It never refers to something that hurts, kills, is ugly, is random, is purposeless, or is otherwise *not good. Towb* is a consistent term, one that is used throughout as a description for good things.

Why would one ever want to make the word mean anything else?

Ultimately, of course, "good" is what is consistent with the character of God, for God is good (Ps. 143:10). Jesus reinforced this attribute in His reply to the young man who called Him good, "Why do you call me good? There is none good but one, that is, God" (Matt. 19:17). Why would someone who believes in the loving God of the Bible want to attribute to that God millions of years of death, suffering, pain, sickness, and survival of the fittest? Can the "good" that God specifically cites be reconciled with the idea of eons of death, pain, suffering, sickness, and survival of the fittest?

Ages of Death and Struggle Defy the Revealed Character of God

Evolutionists ridicule the concept of "day" in Scripture because they need long periods of time to hide the multitude of scientific problems within their view. Time allows them to hide these problems under the bushel of billions of years, far beyond the reach of objective scientific tests. Because Christian compromisers have been so eager and willing to give them the long ages they need, evolutionists do not have to go public with the real focus of their attack: the goodness of God. Those who despise God cannot accept that He is good.

It was not Lyell's long ages that turned Darwin from God; it was the cruel, wasteful, and inefficient struggle for survival that he saw on the Galapagos Islands. Darwin watched as the sea turtles hatched from their sandy nests and made a mad dash for the sea. Then, it seems, he watched in growing horror as perhaps 97 out of 100 were swooped up by predators before they ever got their first taste of salt water. Of the 3 that made it, perhaps 2 were eaten by predators in the sea. Maybe only 1 in 100 survived the first few moments of its life. How, Darwin began to wonder, could such a process be the product of an all-loving, all-powerful God? Some say it was the death of Darwin's own young daughter that finally pushed him completely away from the gospel of Jesus Christ. How could such cruelty exist in a world created on purpose? Who would want to pray to, or ask favors from, a God who would do such things?

It was that heartless and ceaseless struggle for survival, it seems, which began to drive Darwin away from the Creator God. Ironically, Darwin ascribed to God's hand the very processes he at first abhorred. Rather than seeing the different kinds of life as the masterful craftsmanship of the Designer, Darwin came to see living things as the product of *time*, *chance*, *struggle*, and *death*. In his theory of natural selection, Darwin argued that the struggle for survival led to a relentless weeding out and killing off of the weak, paving the way for ever-fitter forms of life to evolve. He summarized this hapless and hopeless view in the closing paragraphs of his *Origin of Species* in these words:

> Thus, from the war of nature, from famine and death, the most exalted object which we are capable of conceiving, namely, the production of higher animals, directly follows. (p. 463)

The "war of nature" became Darwin's substitute for God.

Evolutionary Ages Defy the Revelation of God's Plan and Purpose

Evolutionists have suggested that the difference between evolution and creation should be viewed as the difference between a long series of progressively upward steps contrasted with the belief in a "whimsical" Creator. They have convinced many, including many Christian leaders, that a long series of progressive steps is more logical and scientific than the "whimsical zapper" of the biblical narrative. The real contrasts between creation and evolution, however, are based on the stark difference between *plan and purpose* versus *time and chance* — whether death and struggle are God's means of improvement or a consequence of man's sin.

Evolutionists have also done a terrific job of convincing many, including Christian leaders, that death has always existed and that death has positive value. Death eliminates the weak, improving the quality of a species as a whole, making organisms better and better and fit to more varied environments. Death is the way of removing one generation to make way for another, providing additional opportunities for the expression of "Mother Nature's" creativity — or so the story goes.

Evolution, however, is a horrific process! It is not just a progressive upward development; it is ceaseless struggle and death over endless generations. Even the evolution of cooperation can proceed only over the dead bodies of those that do not cooperate. As Sagan and other evolutionists have always summarized it, the secrets of evolution are *time* and *death*.

For the evolutionists, the fossil record is the showcase for long ages of struggle and death. The mangled bones show evidence of disease and animals ripping each other to shreds. If those fossils are indeed the remains of eons of struggle and death, many must wonder why anyone would want to pray to a God who made so many mistakes, who wiped out over 99 percent of all the species He "created" through this "progressive" evolutionary process.

Eons of Evolutionary Struggle Nullify the Necessity of Christ's Substitutionary Death

When long ages of struggle and death are equaled with the good work of God's creation week, where does Christ fit? Jesus came to conquer death. If, however, long ages of death and struggle are part of God's creativity that He called *very good*, then Jesus winds up opposing God's plan! Jesus, whom the Bible identifies as the Creator, would be blocking the very progress and growth that He used in bringing the world into being. This view would require God taking billions of years of struggle and death to make things all things *very good*, then suddenly deciding that struggle and death was not good. Now, with the change of plans, God would come in the form of Christ to save us from death and to bring in a new heaven and new earth in which death is no more. Notice, by the way, that such reasoning would mean that Christ's return cannot be a *restoration* of all things; for it makes a new heaven and new earth radically different from the first — thus indicating that God changed His mind about what should be called *very good*. Most Christians agree that God can make a new heaven and new earth without death and struggle, completely perfect, "in the twinkling of an eye" (1 Cor. 15:52). That belief is completely incompatible with the idea that He supposedly took billions of years in making a world He once thought was very good but no longer considers that way.

Compromise regarding the length of the creation days calls into question the meaning and authority of God's Word. Compromising with long ages of death and struggle compromises the whole gospel message. If death and struggle were part of God's all-very-good creation, why do we need to be saved from the processes of God's creative work? In such a scenario, Jesus really cannot be our Savior, simply because there is nothing to be saved from. The death and struggle we see now are also considered as always having been part of the world that God created. What is the point then of saving us from what is considered to be God's plan?

Incorporating long ages of death and struggle into God's all-very-good work of creation makes a mockery of the life, work, and words of the Lord Jesus Christ.

God's Gospel Message Is Founded and Framed in His Good Creation

One who understands the gospel message better than many theologians is the *B.C.* cartoonist, Johnny Hart. In one of his cartoons, B.C. is chiseling this poem in stone:

> Often times I wonder what this world is all about.
> It can't be just a place for coming in and going out.
> It surely can't be just a place for terrorists and crooks,
> And dirty, rotten scoundrels that sell pornographic books.
> It [our world] wasn't made for wallowing in sickness, death,
> and sin
> Or people who give drugs to kids, or beat up on their kin.
> Our world was once a perfect place, a gift of love, not war,
> And we still have the power, through grace, to make it
> like before![3]

The poem describes the conditions that we find in our world today. It then goes on to say "our world was once a perfect place, a gift of love, not war." Why did Hart say it that way? According to the Bible, God is love. What did Darwin offer as a substitute for God's love in the origin of all things: it was the war of nature, famine and death. What Johnny Hart is saying through his cartoon strip is that our world was once a perfect place, a gift of (God's) love, not (Darwin's) war. Then he continues "and we still have the power" (in ourselves? No.), "through grace, to make it like before!" WOW! We have a share in Christ's ministry of reconciliation. Are we through the grace of Christ bringing something new into the world that it has never seen before? No, the plan is "to make it like before!" The world God made and called *very good* was a world without *death and struggle*.

Some people, however, might be honestly confused. We seem to live in the world that Darwin described, full of death and struggle. Is that what God wanted? *NO!* Death and struggle are not part of God's creative plan; death and struggle are a result of mankind's sin and rebellion against God.

Something is desperately wrong with our world that needs to be set right. Many other religions blame the bad things in this world on the capriciousness, lust, and power hunger of their gods. Evolutionists prefer to blame it on time and chance, random genetic mistakes culled in a constant and ceaseless struggle for survival. The Bible tells us that struggle, death, disease, and disaster are not in our world as a part of God's original creative acts. Bad things, the Bible teaches, are a direct consequence of mankind's sin, the sin of our first parents, and the sins that continue to be committed by mankind today. The solution to what is desperately wrong is not God's changing His mind about the goodness of death and struggle, as there is certainly no deliverance offered by millions of years of struggle and death until death finally wins. The solution is God's reaching down to mankind through Jesus Christ to restore the relationship that once existed between the Creator and the creature made in His own image.

We have referred often to the passage in Romans 1 by which God tells us that the invisible things of God are clearly seen in all the things that have been made, so clearly that people are without excuse. The revelation of God in nature is not just the vague revelation of some god in general, or some creative force; it is the personal Creator God of the Bible who became flesh and dwelt among us as the Lord Jesus Christ. The world we live in tells us not only about God's eternal power as Creator and sustainer; it also tells us about God's power as Judge and blessed Redeemer. Only the God of the Bible enables us to fully and completely understand the *evidence of His nature in nature around us*.

In the fantastic artistry and intricate engineering design of everything from galaxies to living cells, we see the evidence of God's *supernatural, completed acts as Creator*. We see God as sustainer, the One who daily faithfully maintains His creation, through *continuing, repeatable processes*, the area in which science works so well. Even so, our world is also full of evidence that something has gone wrong; struggle, disease, death, and disaster are a consequence of mankind's sin that brought God's judgment. But, praise God, we also see God's power as Redeemer in the life and work of Jesus Christ, and in the ministry of the Holy Spirit in those who live in a restored relationship with their Maker.

Our Present World

Let us examine now the majestic (not poetic) narrative of Genesis 1 and 2, looking for major contrasts between the world God created *very good* and our present sin-cursed world after Eden.

Perhaps the saddest change in the world after Eden is the severance of the daily, personal communion between the Creator of the universe and His chief stewards and image-bearers. Try to imagine what it was like to walk and talk with the Lord of life in the cool of the day (Gen. 3:8)! People today can take "dust of the ground" (silicon chips) and make things that speak, write, and even check our spelling (those human creations we call computers). No one familiar with computer technology should doubt that God also could form dust of the ground into intelligent creatures, programmed with large vocabularies, ready to converse with the Creator who made them. Computer voice synthesizers do not have to grunt for millions of years before they can speak, and printers do not draw stick figures for eons before they learn to form words and sentences with a grammatical pattern. In an analogous way, God created image-bearers mature and fully operational, with the intelligence and skills they needed to serve as His chief stewards.

Beyond intelligence and skill, however, God created His image bearers with the abilities to love, to care, to fellowship with their Creator, and to worship Him. The creation of Eve elicited a poem of praise from Adam in gratitude to their Creator. No doubt some of those conversations between Adam and his Creator in "the cool of the day" (Gen. 3:8) in Eden concerned the roles and relationships of husband and wife, which God uses throughout Scripture as a picture of His relationship to His people and Christ's relationship to His church. That blessed conversation and communion of mankind with God, of husband and wife, of person with person — a reflection of the discourse among the Trinity — is one of those very good features so distressingly disrupted after Eden.

Some of those God-with-man conversations in the Garden cool may have concerned work! Would people have had work to do in a perfect creation? Contrary to the opinions of many after Eden, the answer is *yes*! Adam and Eve were charged to till and keep the earth (Gen. 2:15). To till is to cultivate, to care for, to nurture, and to bring out the full potential of that which is placed in our charge. Such work, far from being burdensome, is a delight to the soul. Eden means "delight," and mankind's work in Eden was to keep it a Garden of delight. The development of culture, from art to athletics and from literature to the laboratory, is the proper expression of Adam and Eve's so-called cultural mandate. After Eden, joy-giving work became difficult drudgery (Gen. 4:12), and the arts and sciences turned from encouraging mankind and elevating God to defacing man and denigrating the Creator.

The cultural mandate of Genesis 2:15 is also expressed as the dominion mandate in Genesis 1:28: "Have dominion over the fish of the sea, and over the fowl of the air, and over every living thing that moveth upon the earth." The concept of ruling authority and headship earning God's *very good* was turned upside-down after Eden. Jesus had to explain to His followers that it was not to be with them as it was with leaders in our sin-cursed world (Mark 9:35). In our very bad world, authorities lord it over their subjects and take advantage of them; in the "very good" world, the rulers would be servants of all, caring for and cultivating the best in everyone and everything under their authority. That is the biblical concept of "very good" headship which Paul had in mind when he said to men as heads of their families, "Husbands, love your wives, even as Christ also loved the church, and gave himself for it" (Eph. 5:25).

Both the dominion mandate and man's dominion were corrupted by man's sin. Things changed from good to bad in both the exercise of stewardship authority and in the creation itself. After Eden, our mandate was changed from "to till and keep," to following Christ's example "to heal and restore." Everything in the creation is no longer *very good*, there are things wrong that need to be set right. In the spirit of Christ, our ministry of reconciliation is first to lost souls but reconciliation does not stop there. The world God called *very good* has been corrupted by disease, disease organisms, ecological imbalance, and physical infirmity. As Christ brought physical healing, so should we. Recognizing the difference between "good" and "cursed," our stewardship responsibility is not "to keep" tapeworms, malarial parasites, and the AIDS virus, but to help bring healing and restoration by eliminating them.

Evolutionists, environmentalists, and Christian compromisers have trouble with even simple ecological concerns. Evolutionists believe progress occurs when one incipient species expands its niche by killing off the competition, so the preservation of endangered species (i.e., "losers") is anti-evolutionary. However, environmentalists who worship "Mother Nature" believe all organisms (except human beings before birth) are equally entitled to life, yet their bumper stickers inconsistently say "save the whale" and never say "save the tapeworm." Thus, progressive creationists have two problems. First, if God periodically punctuates His world with the creation of new life, the ecological relationship declared "good" on one "day" would be disrupted the next. Second, if death and struggle were part of God's creation at least outside Eden, then why, after Eden, would Jesus heal lepers when the leprosy bacterium was just doing the job God had once called *very good?*

The evolutionist, environmentalist, and progressive creationist cannot understand our world nor act in a manner consistent with their own assumptions. Only the Christian who takes God at His Word can fully appreciate the difference between the good creation of "to till and keep" — using God's infallible guide — and those things gone wrong that are to be healed and restored.

By far the biggest difference between the very good creation and the world after Eden is the intrusion of *death*. "Wherefore, as by one man sin entered into the world, death by sin; and so death passed upon all men" (Rom. 5:12). As discussed further in the next chapter, the Bible describes two kinds of death, spiritual and physical. Spiritual death, the severance of direct and personal communion between the Creator and His image, was instant. Death of the physical body is the culmination of a process that often, before the Flood, stretched beyond 900 years.

Death, of course, is the "last enemy" (1 Cor. 15:26). To conquer death for believers, the God-Man laid down His life, then took it up again (1 John 3:16). In God's good world, Adam and Eve had free access to the tree of life and were created to live. After sin, God drove Adam and Eve from Eden and guarded the way to the tree of life "lest he put forth his hand, and take also of the tree of life, and eat, and live for ever" (Gen. 3:22). In the new heavens and new earth, those restored to new life in Christ will once again have free access to the tree of life (Rev. 22:2).

It is not never-ending life *per se* that God calls good; it is life forever in a vibrant relationship between God's people and their Creator and Redeemer. After Eden, God denied access to the tree of life because He did not want mankind to live forever in sin.

Death so displeased God that He sent His own Son to remove it — not just from mankind, but from the whole of the sin-cursed creation. Romans 8:20–21 tells us how the non-human creation suffered from the willing sin of its steward:

> For the creature was made subject to vanity, not willingly, but by reason of him who hath subjected the same in hope. Because the creature itself also shall be delivered from the bondage of corruption into the glorious liberty of the children of God.

The creation's deliverance is pictured for us in Isaiah 11:6–9:

> The wolf also shall dwell with the lamb, and the leopard shall lie down with the kid; and the calf and the young lion and the fatling together; and a little child shall lead them. And the cow and the bear shall feed; their young ones shall lie down together: and the lion shall eat straw like the ox. And the suckling child shall play on the hole of the asp, and the weaned child shall put his hand on the cockatrice' den. They shall not hurt nor destroy in all my holy mountain: for the earth shall be full of the knowledge of the Lord, as the waters cover the sea.

Christian compromisers cannot rejoice in the promise of Romans 8:20–21 nor in the beautiful picture of the creation's restoration in Isaiah 11:6–9. Progressive creationists, for example, believe God considered long ages of death and struggle among animals to be good — so removing death from the animal world would be removing a good thing, *not* restoring the creation to its created harmony.

God's Good Design for Eating Food

Tied in with the biblical understanding of the goodness of life (and badness of death) is the biblical understanding of diet. The Bible specifically states that God created mankind's parents as vegetarians, giving them every green plant for food (Gen. 1:29–30). Meat lovers need not panic, however, since the Bible also states that, after Eden and more particularly after the Flood (after death had entered the world through sin), God allowed mankind to eat meat (Gen. 9:3), "every moving thing that liveth shall be meat for you: even as the green herb have I given you all things."

Comparison of these two passages make it emphatically clear that the eating of green plants earned God's *very good* commendation, *not* a diet that included animals which ate plants in a "food chain" relationship! Now the temptation to "interpret" rears its ugly head. The same language used to describe the directly vegetarian/herbivorous diet for mankind in Eden is also used to describe the food plan for animals in the pre-sin creation which God called *very good.*

Can it be that *all* animals were created to eat only plants — even bears with big teeth and claws and hawks with hooked bills and sharp talons? Due to the evolutionists' touting Darwin's "war of nature," most people — including many Christian leaders — scoff (or laugh out loud) at the idea of God's good creation being vegetarian. Christian compromisers try to "interpret away" the clear words of Scripture lest they be laughed at as well.

Instead of using currently popular ideas about nature to re-examine God's Word, we should use God's Word to re-examine currently popular ideas about nature.

Asked about carnivorous teeth, a scientist would respond that — in spite of errors echoed by the textbooks, television, museums, and the media — there are no such things as "carnivorous teeth." Over 80 percent of what grizzly bears eat with their "carnivorous teeth," for example, is plant material. The flying fox, a large bat with a mouth and teeth like a fox's, uses its teeth to rip and slash into mangoes and papayas. This diet gives the bat another name — the fruit bat.

The list goes on and on. The popular belief that sharp pointed teeth are "proof" of a carnivorous diet is based on failure in science teaching, success in evolutionary propaganda, or both. The panda looks like a bear, and has teeth and claws like a bear, but it uses this "carnivorous equipment" to eat bamboo. Some evolutionists ran DNA testing hoping to show the panda was really a raccoon, not a bear. The tests came back. It is a bear. What about the claws on a grizzly bear? They can be used to snatch salmon out of a river (or a camper out of his sleeping bag), but they are also used to rake through the ground to dig up meadow lily bulbs, which are prized grizzly food. What about the hooked beak of the hawk? Parrots have hooked beaks more powerful than the hawk's, but they use their sharp talons to pick up seeds, and their strong, hooked beaks to open the seeds. Even the teeth of piranhas that can clean a carcass are used more often to strip the coat from seeds that fall into the Amazon River.

So effective has been the evolutionist's propaganda that even pre-school children given animal figures for play will often start their own "war of nature." Their favorite animals are usually monstrous meat-eating dinosaurs or flesh-tearing sharks! Many children have seen hundreds of hours of terrifying creatures on television before they get to their first Sunday school class. No wonder so many think death, struggle, and animals tearing each other to shreds are normal. The perfect, peaceful, plant-eating creation God called "very good" sounds like a fairy tale that is too good to be true. In reality, it is evolution that is the fairy tale, but it does *not* have a happy ending. Evolution's story is more like one of those wretched Halloween films in which some hideous creature reappears film after film to commit a series of ever more grisly killings.

Unfortunately, there is some basis for evolution's popularity in the world after Eden. Death and struggle, the war of nature, fills the sin-cursed earth. Those who look only at nature might well conclude that death, struggle, and predation have always been, and will always be, part of the natural order of things. But God's Word lifts us above the limits of space and time and gives us a truly eternal perspective that stretches from the beginning to the end of time itself. The spectacles of Scripture, as they have been called, enable us to see beyond the sin-corrupted present to both perfection past (God's very good creation) and perfection future (Christ's return and the new heavens and new earth). This biblical perspective enables one to understand God's revelation of himself in nature as Creator, sustainer, Judge, and blessed Redeemer.

Consider another aspect of predation, for example. The Bible does tell us that God provides prey for the lion (Ps. 104:21), and some Christian leaders say God must have created predators to control animal populations before sin. Predators do play a role in a sin-cursed world, and some animal populations are controlled by predators. Predator populations are, however, controlled by prey populations. When the panther population is high, the deer population will be low, for example. Low deer population then leads to low panther population. Then the cycle is ready to begin anew.

In spite of its effectiveness and its role in God's economy after Eden, the predator-prey population balance is a self-generating, self-regulating cycle that requires no act of creation whatsoever. It is an automatic consequence of some animals killing and eating others. Since many animals with sharp teeth and claws were designed to eat plants, it was only behavior, not anatomy, that changed after Eden. Physiological changes may have occurred additionally as genetic information lost by random mutation degenerated the complex digestive and biochemical systems of herbivores into the much simpler systems of carnivores (in effect "locking in" the behavioral change). Note: it is *not* "scientifically necessary" to blame predator-prey population balance on God, and certainly not desirable theologically to insert this cruel and inefficient process into the creation week about which God called everything *very good.*

God did command the life forms He created to multiply and fill (not overfill) the earth, and scientists have discovered a population control mechanism worthy of God's design that would function, without death, in the good world before sin. It is called territoriality. Territorial population is based on several instincts of "irreducible complexity," including abilities to recognize a territory of the proper size for a mating pair and its offspring, to mark said territory (which is the message of many bird songs) and to defend such territory by "ritualistic combat" (i.e., feather fluttering and singing duels) that involve no death. Once again, science proves to be the Christian's ally in the battle with evolution — and with Christian compromise.

Random mutations could knock out territorial instincts, and the struggle for survival would reward such explosive population tendencies in the short term (which is as far as "natural selection" can "see"). So, an evolutionary process based on mutation-selection (time, chance, struggle, and death) could only destroy territorial population control; it could never create it. As usual, creation explains the good things, and "evolution" explains the bad things.

Note well: scientists looking at God's world through the spectacles of God's Word can explain both the good and the bad, and recognize which things deserve tilling and keeping and which need healing and restoration, that is, which things reflect God's good creation, and which reflect the effects of sin after Eden. Later chapters will show how the spectacles of God's Word give scientists a fruitful head start in understanding God's world — from DNA to the Grand Canyon to starlight and time!

Donning Biblical Glasses

God's Word gives a fruitful head start to the artist and philosopher, as well. One marvelous aspect of God's good creation too often taken for granted is its beauty. Evolution is only about slight advantages in the brutal struggle for survival, and the beauty of God's creation has mystified evolutionists since Darwin. Beauty is usually assigned some utilitarian role in mate attraction, camouflage, or scaring predators — until science shows, as it often does, that the animals do not even see the colors and forms that excite our aesthetic senses. The biblical perspective is given succinctly and sensationally in Genesis 2:9, which says that God created green plants both pleasant to the sight, and good for food. When the struggle boils down to survival, we will eat no matter how the food tastes or looks; but God made good food good tasting and good looking! God even decorated the heavens with stars of many colors, and He created us in His image to find joy and pleasure in beauty. Beauty is definitely a vital part of what God called *very good.*

For philosophers and theologians, perhaps the most perplexing part of God's good creation is the tree of the knowledge of good and evil. It is part of what God called *very good,* so it is good — but how? What makes it good?

The tree was certainly not put there as a temptation, since the Bible tells us God tempts no one. The tree did become the occasion for responsible moral choice, however, as discussed in depth in the next chapter. God could have created people like pets or robots, bred or programmed to give a kind of "love" automatically, without choice. It seems, however, that God chose to create beings with moral choice, and that trait may define us as human beings more than any other; indeed it may be a crucial part of the godhead's image that we bear.

If the tree of knowledge of good and evil shows that God calls moral choice good, then the Creator's goodness infinitely exceeds the goodness of His creation. When our first parents sinned, God sent His own Son to pay the penalty for their wrong choice, and we see the transcendent goodness of God in Jesus Christ's love for the unlovely. In heaven, His nail-pierced hands will demonstrate the greatest good forever!

What Does the Character of God Demand?

If one of the functions of the creation is instruction in the nature of God (Rom. 1:20) and speaking the universal language of God's glory (Ps. 19:1–3), then should we not expect the message to be both understandable and accurate? Turn the question around. If the story of the creation is *not* understandable or accurate, then what would that tell us about the God who claims to have created it? If the Bible reveals one kind of God, and creation (nature) another, which one do we believe? If the message of salvation preaches the good news of an omnipotent, omniscient God who became man to rescue us; yet if we find that He has misrepresented himself in language of His own choosing, then what are we to think about the character of such a Savior?

Everything that we know about the God of the Bible indicates that He is "not the author of confusion" (1 Cor. 14:33). Rather, every word God utters has a purpose and plan behind it (Isa. 55:11). The Bible absolutely insists on verbal accuracy — that *every word* of God is precisely the word that God wants to record (Prov. 30:5). Some may not believe this, but the Bible is consistent. There is no question that Jesus Christ used God's writings with a precision that included even the tenses of the verbs. Anything short of "the truth, the whole truth, and nothing but the truth," we know to be a lie!

What about the thrice-holy character of God? If ever there were an axiomatic statement about what God is, it would have to be the "holy, holy, holy" attribute that is eternally murmured from the lips of the living creatures surrounding the throne of God (Isa. 6:3; Rev. 4:8). Can God, whose very essence is holiness, lie? No, of course not! Nothing about the Creator can be a "lie" (Num. 23:19; Titus 1:2). What utter foolishness to believe in a Holy God whom we absolutely trust for our eternal destiny, and yet believe that He would muddle His own account of creation.

What does the Bible teach about omniscience? The Bible often describes God as all-knowing and all-seeing. Jesus taught that the Father in heaven knows even when a small bird dies, and that He has specific knowledge of the number of hairs on our heads (Matt. 10:29–30). Was He not telling us in practical and everyday language how complete the knowledge of God really is? When the Psalmist sang about the unlimited knowledge of the God who knew the name of each star (Ps. 147:4) was he being merely poetic or was he revealing something about the infinite knowledge of the Creator?

Is it at all possible for the God of all knowledge to experiment? Would that not be a negation of omniscience? If the creation account is to be understood in the terms of naturalistic explanations, if we are to interpret the words of Genesis to coincide with the non-directed progress of evolutionary development, then we are compelled to believe in a God who would allow eons of death and random mutations. If this indeed has happened, then obvious questions arise. How could an omniscient God permit, or even use, the most inefficient, horrific, random biological process imaginable and then step in from time to time with a good event? How could God, who is life, defy His very nature and use death to create life forms? The two concepts are mutually exclusive.

The revelation that we have been given about God (remember, it is revelation — Deut. 29:29) is that He can *do* nothing but *perfect* works (Ps. 18:30). Given the absolutely contradictory messages of a long-age evolutionary randomness and the omniscient perfect actions of a Holy God, one would have to conclude that either the information we have about God is incorrect, and therefore deceptive, or it is absolutely right. It is not possible to have partially complete omniscience; it would be better to reject the idea of God and ignore the biblical record of creation altogether. At least that position is consistent with human logic. To embrace a belief that an omniscient God would design randomness is nonsense.

What Does the "Good" in Creation Teach Us?

We learn two facts about the creation from other places in the Bible. First, the Creator is none other than Jesus of Nazareth, the Word made flesh.

- In the beginning was the Word, and the Word was with God, and the Word was God. The same was in the beginning with God. All things were made by him; and without him was not any thing made that was made (John 1:1–3).
- But to us there is but one God, the Father, of whom are all things, and we in him; and one Lord Jesus Christ, by whom are all things, and we by him (1 Cor. 8:6).
- For by him were all things created, that are in heaven, and that are in earth, visible and invisible, whether they be thrones, or dominions, or principalities, or powers: all things were created by him, and for him (Col. 1:16).
- God, who at sundry times and in divers manners spake in time past unto the fathers by the prophets, Hath in these last days spoken unto us by his Son, whom he hath appointed heir of all things, by whom also he made the worlds (Heb. 1:1–2).

- And, Thou, Lord, in the beginning hast laid the foundation of the earth; and the heavens are the works of thine hands (Heb. 1:10).
- Thou art worthy, O Lord, to receive glory and honour and power: for thou hast created all things, and for thy pleasure they are and were created (Rev. 4:11).

The One who hung on the cross for our sins is the One who spoke the heavens and the earth into existence. The One who uttered the incomprehensible "Father, forgive them; for they know not what they do" is the One who created man in His own image (Luke 23:34). The One who rose from the dead is the One who created life. What we see (and many profess to believe) about Jesus Christ must be inseparably interwoven with the actions of the Creator. All of the attributes of Jesus Christ that give us the hope for our salvation — love, mercy, grace, compassion, and forgiveness — all of them must be present in the *acts* of the Creator-Savior. Can He *be* love and also consciously perform that which randomly kills, maims, and tortures? Can He *be* merciful and also be indifferent to suffering?

Jesus Christ and His nature are inextricably tied to creation.

Second, the creation record reveals the nature of God. Many passages emphasize this critical point:

- The heavens declare the glory of God; and the firmament sheweth his handywork. Day unto day uttereth speech, and night unto night sheweth knowledge. There is no speech nor language, where their voice is not heard (Ps. 19:1–3).
- Because that which may be known of God is manifest in them; for God hath shewed it unto them. For the invisible things of him from the creation of the world are clearly seen, being understood by the things that are made, even his eternal power and Godhead; so that they are without excuse (Rom. 1:19–20).

- When I consider thy heavens, the work of thy fingers, the moon and the stars, which thou hast ordained; What is man, that thou art mindful of him? and the son of man, that thou visitest him? (Ps. 8:3–4).
- Let all the earth fear the LORD: let all the inhabitants of the world stand in awe of him. For he spake, and it was done; he commanded, and it stood fast (Ps. 33:8–9).
- To whom then will ye liken me, or shall I be equal? saith the Holy One. Lift up your eyes on high, and behold who hath created these things, that bringeth out their host by number: he calleth them all by names by the greatness of his might, for that he is strong in power; not one faileth (Isa. 40:25–26).
- For as I passed by, and beheld your devotions, I found an altar with this inscription, TO THE UNKNOWN GOD. Whom therefore ye ignorantly worship, him declare I unto you. God that made the world and all things therein, seeing that he is Lord of heaven and earth, dwelleth not in temples made with hands; Neither is worshipped with men's hands, as though he needed any thing, seeing he giveth to all life, and breath, and all things (Acts 17:23–25).

The passages above are samplings of many such teachings throughout the Bible. Because God is the Creator, He is sovereign, He is able, He is the law, He is the hope, and He is the Savior. Everything about the message of Scripture rests on this foundational beginning — that God created the heavens and the earth. Since it is God who created, everything about the creation was good.

Everything God Did Was Good

The summary statement in Genesis 1:31 encapsulates all that had transpired in the six days during which God created the heaven and the earth. Nothing about the end product was bad. Nothing about the way the universe functioned, nothing about the way the environment worked, nothing about the way the life-breathers related, nothing about His stewards — nothing was *"un-good."*

How could it be otherwise? If God is omnipotent and omniscient, how could He make a mistake or fail or not remember? A holy God could not author *un-good.* If God intended the creation to speak His glory, then He must have made it in such a way that the creatures could understand the message. To ignore the clear teachings of so much of Scripture is to ignore the God of the Scripture and to reject the message of the Scripture.

All his works are done in truth (Ps. 33:4).

Endnotes

1 David L. Hull, "The God of the Galapagos," review of *Darwin on Trial*, by Philip Johnson, *Nature*, 352 (August 8, 1991): 485-486.

2 Charles Darwin, *Origin of Species*, text from the 6th ed. 1882 (London: J.M. Dent & Sons Ltd., 1928), p. 463.

3 Johnny Hart, "B.C." (Creator's Syndicate Inc., distributed by L.A. Times Syndicate, 1989).

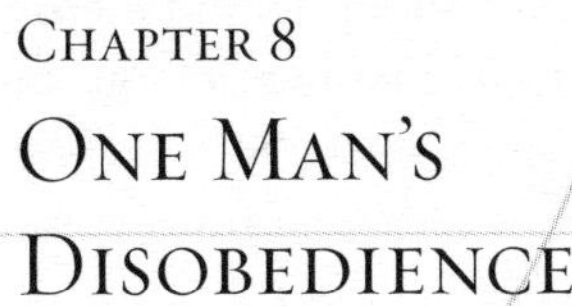

Chapter 8
One Man's Disobedience

That is why the world is in such a state today.[1]

— King Mswati of Swaziland, blaming "women who wear pants" for the worlds ills.

Genesis 3 is much like a breaking story in a news broadcast. God has just finished announcing His program and design for the universe. Adam has given his first-hand account of what he experienced and has told us all about the Garden of Eden and its delightful environment. One can almost picture the imaginary television backdrop. The somber-faced news anchor is standing in front of a magnificent walled entrance to a green, tree-lined estate stretching off into the distance. Sizzling next to the gated entrance are two "beings" whose fire-like brilliance makes the cameramen blink and the news anchor very nervous.

Every few seconds an off-camera "swish" is heard when something from the "entities" slices through the area around the gate. The object is too quick to catch with the lens, but the sound it makes is frighteningly like a sword cutting through the air. The news anchor glances down at the papers, stares carefully at the camera, and says something like, "This is what we know so far. Adam and Eve have been barred from Eden for violating their contract with the owner. They are presently in seclusion at an undisclosed location somewhere south of Eden, but they have not as yet spoken with reporters. The only other witness to these events, the serpent, is quite distraught and unwilling to talk to reporters."

"The creatures you see behind me are officially called 'cherubim' and are senior members of the owner's entourage. They have been given orders to keep everyone out of the Garden and especially to prevent anyone from gaining access to the fabled 'tree of life.' *Elohim* has not yet revealed His plans about the contract dispute, but is widely known for His personal generosity as well as His legal precision. As soon as we learn more, we will keep you informed. Now back to our regular programming."

The Good Creation Declares God's Glory

God pronounced His creation work, "Very good." Every word, every line — even the very grammatical structure of these accounts (Gen. 1–2) — is designed to provide a clear, unobstructed record of what has been done. Given the economy of words (only 670 Hebrew words comprise the entire section), one can hardly conceive of any other words that could have been used to make the obvious meaning more obvious. This universe was designed and created by God to make the invisible nature of the triune Creator clearly seen by its human inhabitants. All life breathers as well as the earth itself have been put under the authority of Adam and his helpmeet, both of whom are to fill the earth with their progeny.

Everything in the newly created *good* environment had the potential for good relationships and a good future. The universe is carefully regulated so that the passage of time is visible and understood, and earth is ruled by the greater and lesser lights. Sufficient food and shelter is being produced to provide for all living things. Boundaries have been set both for physical earth systems and living kinds. All living creatures are functioning under laws of reproductive design that not only circumscribe their behavior but also ensure their success. The two stewards are placed in a specially prepared garden with the broadest of liberties and are given face to face access to the Creator with whom they fellowship.

Given great liberty and the grand goodness of creation, Adam and Eve are only restricted from the knowledge of evil. They are certainly encouraged to know the good things of creation. They are granted liberty to experience the goodness of the Garden. They are afforded the fellowship of the Creator and the intimacy of each other. They are finished; they are complete; they are good.

The whole of God's Word — and God's world — pivots on Genesis 3.

History Is Changed by Rebellion

Enter the serpent.

Genesis 3:1 gives little information about the serpent, but there is absolutely no change in the tone or style of the writings. The author of Genesis is quite clear that this account is to be viewed with the same historicity as the previous information. There is no linguistic reason to "insert" an allegorical abstract into the text.

It is most likely that the chief angel, Lucifer, in some way took over this serpent (*nachash*) for purposes of disguise. Revelation gives Satan the title "serpent" (20:2) and identifies him in serpent form (12:9-15) as the power behind the beast that rules the world. Paul cites the incident in the Garden (2 Cor. 11:3) as actual history and warns that our minds can be deceived just as Eve's mind was beguiled. Whatever this living creature looked like in its created form, it was radically changed when God passed sentence on its behavior.

Lucifer was created with perfection and complete holiness and was, apparently, afforded privileges unique among the angelic host — even to the walking with liberty among "the stones of fire" and freedom to be on "the holy mountain of God." Scripture specifically states that Lucifer was in "Eden, the Garden of God" and was magnificently adorned with priceless jewels (Ezek. 28:13–16). It is clearly obvious that Lucifer was exceedingly privileged and supernaturally endowed.

The Scriptures tell us that Lucifer "said in [his] heart" that he would exalt his throne above the stars of God and that he made an attempt to "be like the most high" (Isa. 14:12–15). Jesus said that Satan (Lucifer) is the father of lies and a murderer from the beginning (John 8:44). Since Lucifer was created in perfection — since the godhead pronounced all of creation "good" — the attempt at usurpation and the fathering of lies and the murder must have taken place after God had pronounced everything that He had created and made as "very good" and after Adam sinned (Gen. 1:31–2:3). Therefore, the indictment made by Jesus (the Creator and the One who spoke the initial benediction on creation) must have spoken of a condition that applied to Satan *after* his creation, *after* the benediction on creation, but *before* Genesis 3. Thus, Satan's fall could not have occurred between Genesis 1:1 and 1:2 nor at any time during the creation week.

Adam and Eve were obviously in the Garden for some span of time, but it is not possible to read eons of time into the period between chapters 2 and 3. God had commanded Adam and Eve to "fill the earth" with their children. There is no evidence of any children before Cain and no reason to ignore other children if they existed prior to chapter 3. If such children indeed existed, they would have retained the genetic and spiritual purity of Adam and Eve in their holiness and would have presented a doctrinal difficulty unknown in the biblical record. Eve first conceives after she and Adam have been expelled from the garden (Gen. 4:1). Still so fresh in her mind were the concluding events in Eden that she names their son "Cain" (the "received one" or "acquired one") to commemorate the promise given by the Creator (Gen. 3:15).

Satan's Lie Fathers the Rebellion

Satan (Lucifer) had chosen to rebel against the Creator. Through this event he "fathered" the lie. We are not given much biblical information about that event; but perhaps Lucifer may have thought, since he appeared in a fully developed state with such power and glory, that he was created by nothing more than a confluence of energy — and the same, according to his reasoning, might also be true of *Elohim*. *Elohim* was in power, therefore, only by accident, a quirk in order of appearance. If both were the result of blind energy coming to consciousness, Lucifer could believe he deserved to rule as much as *Elohim*. The privilege and power of the throne of God should and could be his.

Regardless of the accuracy of that speculation, the Bible does clearly teach us that Lucifer, not the Creator, is the source of lies (John 8:44; Titus 1:2). Lucifer must have even believed his own lie. He instigated rebellion in heaven, then brought his lies to earth. Unfortunately, many passages imply that Satan still has great authority and much liberty both in heaven and on earth (Job 1:6–12, 2:1–7; Matt. 12:26; Acts 5:3, 26:18; 1 Cor. 5:5; 2 Cor. 2:11, 11:14; 2 Tim. 2:26; 1 Pet. 5:8; Rev. 2:13).

Satan Devises a War Strategy To Compromise Man

It *is* clear from Scripture that Satan is focused on deceiving mankind (2 Cor. 4:4, 11:3) by twisting and distorting the truth of God into a lie in order to ultimately build an army of humanity to fight against the Creator (Rev. 20:8). His three-fold battle strategy is exposed in the serpent's conversation with Eve.

• Initiate DOUBT about the accuracy or authority of God's Word (Gen. 3:1).

Satan decided to introduce doubt at the very simplest level: the level of the Word. Whether doubt comes by intellect or by experience, doubt is absolutely vital to the eradication of confidence in God. Doubt in the truthfulness, doubt in the accuracy, doubt in the authenticity, doubt in the hearing, doubt in the seeing, and doubt in the knowing — all serve to destroy the effect of God's Word. This is the first stage of Satan's strike since "faith cometh by hearing, and hearing by the word of God" (Rom. 10:17). Eve was asked a simple question ("Did God say?") that served to plant in her mind the possibility that God either did not say something or that she had misunderstood what God had said. Doubt brings instability to one's mind and to one's faith (James 1:5–8). Doubt is both very powerful and very subtle. Doubt is strategy number one.

• Introduce DENIAL of the capacity of God to perform His Word (Gen. 3:4).

Denial is the underlying character trait of the ungodly people identified as representing the last days (2 Tim. 3:1–5): denial of the power of God; denial of the capability of God to do what He said He would do; denial of the possibility that the Word of God can even be true. They deny the words. They deny the thoughts. They deny the implications of the concepts. Satan confronted Eve with a direct denial that God would (or could) not do as He promised ("Ye shall not surely die"). With her faith weakened by doubt, she began to entertain the possibility that God was in some way impotent. Denial is strategy number two.

• Impute DENIGRATION to the character of God himself (Gen. 3:5).

Ultimately, Satan desires to attribute to God the self-centered evil of Satan's own character and to lead us to make God into a creature rather than the Creator (Rom. 1:21–25). Eve was told that God was deceiving her and was withholding from her that which would allow her to obtain the same knowledge as the Creator, thus making her equal with God. Eve would never have considered the truthfulness of Satan's statement, if her faith had not been weakened by doubt and undermined by the denial of God's omnipotence. Once man doubts, once he accepts denial of God's power, it becomes easy to denigrate the very character of God. A god whose word cannot be trusted, a god who will not (or cannot) keep his word, is not worthy of worship. Once our minds question the power of God, it becomes a natural flow of logic to attribute a lie in one form or another to the character of God. Denigration is strategy number three.

While the tactics and circumstances are infinitely varied, the strategy remains the same. From this point forward in the biblical text, there is continual conflict with Lucifer, whose efforts to undermine and control the events of history center around his strategic plan to introduce doubt into God's Word, promote denial of God's power or authority, and encourage man to denigrate God's character.

Eve Is Deceived and Capitulates

Eve's conversation with the serpent is recorded for our instruction. Many have drawn multiple conclusions from these few verses, but it is clear that Eve's behavior is to be considered a classic human response (2 Cor. 11:3).

- **Eve misapplied or misunderstood God's Word (Gen. 3:3).**

Initially, Eve left a portion of God's Word either unsaid or unknown. God specifically told Adam and Eve that they could freely eat of all the other trees in the Garden. Eve either failed to note the generosity of God or thought it to be of no consequence. Then, Eve added her own emphasis — "neither shall you touch it" — to the words of God, and softened (one might say, interpreted) God's command from "ye shall surely die" to "lest you (might) die." Both the subtraction and addition errors are warned against in later passages (Deut. 12:32; Josh. 1:7; Prov. 30:6; Matt. 5:18; Rev. 22:18–19).

If we are not to succumb to the same fault, we must hide God's Word in our hearts (Ps. 119:11). We give an advantage to the enemy when we change any of the words of God (Deut. 12:32). Our responsibility is to know and believe the words (Prov. 22:19–21) and not to twist the words (2 Pet. 1:20).

- **Eve failed to rebuke, resist, or even question the serpent.**

Godly believers are told that they are to resist Satan in the faith and that open defiance of Satan's lie will cause him to flee (James 4:7; 1 Pet. 5:9). Three of the Gospel accounts tell of Jesus resisting Satan in the wilderness (Matt. 4; Mark 1; Luke 4). On every occasion, Satan tested Jesus using a distortion or faulty interpretation of biblical truth. Jesus resisted by accurately quoting the words of God. Eve did nothing of the kind.

Satan is master of the half-truth and can disguise his approach in the light (2 Cor. 11:14). The *half-light* of half-truth will dissipate only when we shine the light of the glorious gospel (2 Cor. 4:4) on the lies. When we remain passive, we become victims. When we turn the power of truth on the lie, we are set free (John 8:32).

• **Eve failed to seek counsel or assert obedience.**

Eve should have rejected Satan's lie. All was now clear — believe the serpent or believe God. Yet, she did not turn to Adam for advice or counsel or assert her responsibility to obey her Creator and Lord. By her silence, self-sufficiency, and reticence to obey God, she allowed herself to be deceived into open disobedience (Rom. 6:16).

If we would not mimic her sin, we must desire the pure milk of Scripture (1 Pet. 2:2) and exercise our minds so that we can tell the difference between good and evil (Heb. 5:14). When events and challenges exceed our knowledge and ability to resist, we must seek safety in the wisdom of a multitude of counselors (Prov. 11:14).

• **Eve displays the prototype behavior of all those who embrace Satan's lie.**

Below are things Satan uses to lure us away from holiness (1 John 2:15–16):

- The object is attractive physically.
- The action is attractive esthetically.
- The result promises mental superiority.

In this case, the forbidden fruit was "good for food." However, Adam and Eve had no need, no hunger — they had access to all other fruits. The fruit was "pleasant to the eyes," but Eve was surrounded by beauty in a garden planted by God's own hand. She was drawn away to the minor beauty of the moment. Then Eve focused on an action that is "desired to make one wise." How foolish! She had perfect knowledge of good and daily fellowship with God. Her self-deception blinded her from the wonder of her personal relationship with the Creator — all for the possibility of learning some supposed secret that would make her "like" God. She had forgotten or discarded the fact that she already possessed the image of God.

Remarkably, Satan's challenge to Eve, and his challenge to Christians today, is directed at clear, simple concepts expressed in clear, simple words — words like eat, fruit, six, days, death, and sin. The correct God-glorifying response is often a simple "yes" or "no." Satan did not ask Eve to explain how God could claim to get light from distant stars to the earth on the same day they were created. Similarly, Satan does not challenge Christians today with questions about the subtleties of Pauline doctrine. Instead, he asks simple questions about simple words that can be simply answered — IF we have child-like faith and trust that the words challenged are the clear, simple words of our loving omniscient, omnipotent heavenly Father.

A simple, direct, correct answer would "expose" us as children trusting their Father's words. No advanced degrees are required; no hermeneutical gymnastics are needed; all that is required is just trusting faith based on who God is — the kind of faith that any human being could have, regardless of IQ or number of books published or number of languages spoken.

For some, including Eve, that is not enough. Satan continued his challenge by suggesting that God did not really mean what He said. God had told Adam that by eating the one forbidden fruit "thou shalt surely die" (Gen. 2:17). The serpent said to Eve, "Ye shall not surely die" (Gen. 3:4). By allowing herself to go this far, Eve now had to make a choice. "Do I take God's Word literally, or can I interpret it to mean something else?"

Like Christians who follow her example today, Eve decided that her intelligence could sit in judgment of God's Word. Using the tools of science, her brain and her senses, Eve began examining the evidence for herself. No poison dripped from the forbidden fruit; no harmful spines protruded from it. It delighted the eyes as much or more than any other fruit in the Garden. In her opinion, God's severe warning about the fruit was not supported by her own "scientific analysis," so an interpretation beyond the literal meaning of God's words must be sought.

Then came Satan's subtlest and most appealing challenge. With Eve already questioning God's simple words and believing in her intelligence to decide the issue, Satan only had to suggest that by eating the fruit; "ye shall be as gods." When Eve concluded the tree "to be desired to make one wise, she took of the fruit thereof, and did eat" (Gen. 3:6). Like too many Christians today, Eve found the temptation to be wise in her own eyes irresistible and thus subjugated God's words to her knowledge and wisdom. Eve may really have convinced herself that God secretly wanted her to eat the forbidden fruit, so that she would become like God, capable of engaging in adult give-and-take with her Creator, elevating the plane of their fellowship to a mature level far above the child-Father relationship. After all, God really did give us free moral choice. Would He not then want us to use our intelligence?

Of course, God wants us to use intelligence He gave us. He wants us to understand His Word and apply it to an expanding horizon of discoveries and knowledge. The greatest minds have considered it a noble challenge "to think God's thoughts after Him." After all these millennia, theologians have still not plumbed the depths of the Greatest Book Ever Written.

God did not intend, of course, that we should use our intelligence to question His words, His authority, His wisdom, or His love. How foolish it is to put the words of human experts above the Word of the transcendent Creator! Why should we want to trust the words of men who were not there at the beginning, finite men who do not know everything, men who have made lots of mistakes? Would it not be more intelligent to accept the Word of the God who was there at the beginning, the infinite One who does know everything, who never makes mistakes — and who loves us deeply?

That last question would be rhetorical, obviously answered "yes," except for three things: the lust of the flesh, the lust of the eyes, and the pride of life. Like mother; like child. We, like Eve, find it too easy to become puffed up with our own wisdom. Many would rather bask in the praises of men than earn their Creator's "well done, thou good and faithful servant." Worse yet, too many also hide their faith under a bushel, afraid to stand on God's Word because they cannot stand up to the put-downs of those who are wise in their own eyes.

Eve reasoned from the flesh (Rom. 8:5–8) rather than from the spirit, and *she reasoned herself to death.* She loved "the things that are in the world" (1 John 2:15–17) rather than the "things above" (Col. 3:2). Once fallen, she wanted a companion to mimic her choice (Rom. 1:32; 1 Cori. 15:33). All of us follow this pattern when we open ourselves to the lies of Lucifer.

Adam's Rebellion Is Deliberate, Wicked, and Inexcusable

Scripture clearly indicates that Adam was not deceived (1 Tim. 2:14). Adam's defiance is cited as the reason he bears the responsibility for sin's entrance into the world. *This open and conscious rebellion,* not Eve's, is what brings God's subsequent judgment on the world (Rom. 5:12–19). Adam was at least nearby during the entire incident (Gen. 3:6), yet his first response upon being confronted with his rebellion was to blame God for the problem (Gen. 3:12).

Some commentators have tried to make Adam out to be a self-sacrificing, loving type of Christ. That is, Adam knowingly took the fruit from Eve's hand because he loved her and did not want her to die without him — or perhaps he thought that if he took of the forbidden fruit, God would blame him and not Eve. Rubbish! Not only does Scripture specifically state that Adam was not deceived, but it also lays the entire blame for the judgment of God and the subsequent burden of mankind completely at the feet of Adam. There was no sacrificial love given here; there was only rebellion. There was no maudlin pity for Eve; there was blatant insubordination.

Adam took no steps to instruct or correct Eve. Some have suggested that she was not present when God gave the specific command to Adam in the Garden and that Eve was somewhat ignorant of what God wanted. Even if that were so (and it is not at all clear that that is the case), Adam knew full well what was transpiring. Adam had no excuse. None! He knew precisely what God had forbidden, allowed his helpmeet to listen to the lies of the serpent, and then stood by while *she reasoned herself to death.* Perhaps, some have thought, if Adam could see no effect of the disobedience on Eve, he would have bought into the lie and participated with her. That action would have made Adam's sin even more heinous! If that were so, he used Eve to experiment with God's judgment — risked her life — before he risked his. Thus, Adam — and only Adam — became the cause of God's severe and just judgment on the creation placed under Adam's dominion. Death would now reign until the great Redeemer entered His created world to conquer death with the grace of His incomprehensible atonement on the Cross (Rom. 5:17–21).

Rejection of Personal Responsibility and Guilt

Display of independent rebellion by our first parents in the Garden explains much about human nature. "Passing the buck" is a favorite human pastime. Even serial killers seek sympathy and understanding by blaming their crimes (and their choices) on society, a bully at school, poverty, a mother working two jobs, drug dealers, environmental pollution, or, ultimately, God. It started in the Garden. When questioned by God, Adam blamed his actions on his wife ("whom thou gavest to be with me"), shifting the real blame to God himself (Gen. 3:12)! Eve blamed the "serpent [who] beguiled me" (Gen. 3:13); and, as the old joke goes, the serpent did not have a leg to stand on.

If there is an all-pervasive characteristic of humanity, it is to cast blame on anything and anyone other than ourselves. One famous comedian built his career on the slogan, "The devil made me do it." We laugh at the antics but cry over the reality. Court cases are won or lost on blame for guilt. Wars are fought, families broken, reputations made or destroyed — all in an effort to avoid or to cast blame. The record of Genesis is absolutely indicative of human reality.

This is entirely the point. Guilt sets humanity apart, for it is the universal acknowledgment that all men know when wrong is done (Rom. 2:15). Guilt underlies human effort to seek happiness. Humanistic psychiatry strives to eliminate the idea of guilt, but psychiatrists themselves have one of the highest suicide rates of any profession. Animals do not harbor guilt. They may express avoidance behavior when they are aware of pending punishment, but they do not share this human characteristic.

God gave Adam only one prohibition: do not eat of the fruit of the tree of the knowledge of good and evil. With the fruit came the knowledge of evil. When the thought of disobedience became action, guilt entered into the human psyche. It remains there until purged by the Creator.

Human Susceptibility to Deception Is Confirmed

The conversation between the serpent and Eve reveals humanity's susceptibility to the deception of untruth. The Scripture repeatedly warns humanity against such vulnerability (Ps. 10 and 37; 2 Cor. 11:3; 2 Tim. 3:13). God's nature is truth and life (John 14:6). Satan's character is lies and death (John 8:44). When Eve allowed herself to be led into deception, she displayed the essence of a self-centered logic that, if followed, will always stray from God's supernatural holiness and omniscience. Focusing on the physical aspects alone (good for food), limited by the observable facts only (was pleasant to the eyes), and compounded by the selfish desire for mental superiority (desired to make one wise), Eve capitulated to the deception of Lucifer.

Nothing has changed since then. Whenever we focus on the temporal things to the exclusion of the unseen things of eternity (2 Cor. 4:18), our minds are blinded (2 Cor. 4:4). That deception is hostile to truth. Whenever we exclude faith from our reasoning, we become the victims of deception just as Eve became deceived (2 Cor. 11:3). The beguiling words of man's human logic and naturalistic philosophy will spoil us just as surely today as it spoiled our parents in Eden (Col. 2:4–8).

> By one man's disobedience many were made sinners (Rom. 5:19).

Endnotes

1 King Mswati, quoted in Perspectives, *Newsweek*, June 9, 2003, p. 23.

CHAPTER 9

CURSED IS THE GROUND

The last thing that I've been unable to control in my quest to control everything around me is death.[1]

— Metallica drummer Lars Ulrich

Where Do Death, Pain, and Suffering Come From?

How would you answer a neighbor who angrily tells you, "I have a cousin dying from the AIDS virus, and a mother with Alzheimer's that does not even know me. My daughter's house was destroyed by a tornado, and my only grandson was killed. Now the EPA is making me move from the house I have lived in all my life because some underground ore deposit is filling it with radioactive radon. Where is this Creator-God of love and power you Christians are always talking about?"

What do you say — "Have a nice day"? There really are things terribly wrong with the world after Eden. Many people blame those horrors on the God of the Bible; the Bible blames them on the sin of mankind. God is the source of what is good in our world; mankind's sin is the source of what is bad. In a world terrified by terrorists, Christians need to be able to explain what it means to live in a corrupted creation.

The previous chapter described the nature of sin, and how sin brought instant spiritual death (severing mankind's personal relationship with God) and progressive physical death. Sin did not stop at ruining man's relationship with the Creator; sin also ruined the creation. Death extends not only to the children of Adam and Eve but also to all the animals originally put under their care. According to Hebrews 1:10–11 and Psalm 102:25–26, the death principle (disintegration of ordered systems) extends even to the ends of the created cosmos:

> They [the heavens] shall perish; but thou remainest; and they all shall wax old as doth a garment (Heb. 1:11).

How could one man's disobedience have such far-reaching and devastating consequences?

Cursed Is the Ground for Your Sake (Gen. 3:17)

For being deceived into sinning (so easily, it seems), Eve is punished with pain in childbearing and a submissive relationship to the husband whose counsel she did not seek. Adam's punishment was astronomically greater, befitting (1) his far greater sin of willfully chosen rebellion; and (2) his role as chief steward of God's creation, the one who named the animals God created.

> And unto Adam he said . . . cursed is the ground for thy sake (Gen. 3:17).

It was not Adam's body that bore the penalty for his sin; it was the ground, the very substance of which the material universe was made, the very elements God had molded to form his body and those of the other living creatures. The punishment for Adam's sin extended as far as the matter of which he was made and as far as the dominion with whose care he was charged. God takes human beings, and human sin, very seriously!

Some say Adam's sin affected only the spiritual nature of man and perhaps brought on his physical death. The Bible teaches something radically different! The effect of the curse on the botanical world is explicitly stated by God when He announced Adam's punishment: "Thorns also and thistles shall it bring forth to thee; and thou shalt eat the herb of the field; In the sweat of thy face shalt thou eat bread, till thou return unto the ground; for out of it wast thou taken: for dust thou art, and unto dust shalt thou return" (Gen. 3:18–19).

Romans 8:20–23 describes how the penalty for man's sin, the curse on the ground, affects the whole of non-human creation. "For the creature [creation] was made subject to vanity, not willingly, but by reason of him who hath subjected the same in hope" (Rom. 8:20).

Note several points made in this verse:

- "For the creature [creation] was made subject to vanity, not willingly. . . ." The creation did not sin; man did. Man was a sinner "willingly." That which was subjected "not willingly" is not human creation, which God endowed with will and moral choice, but the non-human creation.
- The creation was "subject to vanity," an excellent description of the time and chance upon which evolution is based. Evolutionists believe that time and chance ultimately lead to progressive development of greater order. The Bible teaches, and science confirms, that time and chance destroy order. As a process of time, chance, struggle, and death, evolution is real enough in a sin-cursed world; but those evolutionary processes do not create — they corrupt. Indeed, Romans 1:21 states that the present, fallen creation is in a "bondage of corruption."

Even as it tells us that the cursed creation is in a "bondage of corruption," Romans 1:21 (building on the last two words in Rom. 1:20) points toward the glorious restoration in which the non-human creation shares "in hope, because the creature [creation] itself also shall be delivered from the bondage of corruption into the glorious liberty of the children of God."

The promise of restoration for both man and man's original dominion (the creation) are restated in Romans 8:22–23:

> For we know that the whole creation groaneth and travaileth in pain together until now. And not only they, but ourselves also, which have the firstfruits of the Spirit, even we ourselves groan within ourselves, waiting for the adoption, to wit, the redemption of our body.

The extent of the curse is also clearly evident in the extent of the restoration, 2 Peter 3:7, 10–13:

> But the heavens and the earth, which are now, by the same word are kept in store, reserved unto fire against the day of judgment and perdition of ungodly men. . . . But the day of the Lord will come as a thief in the night; in the which the heavens shall pass away with a great noise, and the elements shall melt with fervent heat, the earth also and the works that are therein shall be burned up. Seeing then that all these things shall be dissolved, what manner of persons ought ye to be in all holy conversation and godliness, looking for and hasting unto the coming of the day of God, wherein the heavens being on fire shall be dissolved, and the elements shall melt with fervent heat? Nevertheless we, according to his promise, look for new heavens and a new earth, wherein dwelleth righteousness.

If Adam's sin affected only mankind, why would God replace an *all-very-good* earth with a new earth? If Adam's sin affected only the earth, why would God make new heavens? The Bible has the answer in the verses above. The penalty for Adam's sin was the *curse on the ground*, the elemental basis for the whole physical universe. Therefore, as 2 Peter 3:12 states, "the elements shall melt with fervent heat." The effects of Adam's sin are purged when "the heavens being on fire shall be dissolved." Because the effect of Adam's sin was cosmic in scope, the restoration is cosmic in scope: a "new heavens and a new earth, wherein dwelleth righteousness."

What Is Death?

God decreed that should Adam violate the one restriction placed on him by his Creator, then Adam would surely die on that very day. The observable effects of that fateful day were less than what natural reasoning might suppose. Should we hear a sentence like that today, we would expect an immediate execution. However, from a physical viewpoint, not much appeared to happen. Neither Adam nor Eve dropped dead. Was God lying? Did He not mean what He said? That question was exactly what the serpent had asked Eve. Was the serpent right?

Death is the most serious consequence of Adam's sin, and the final enemy (1 Cor. 15:26). People have an intuitive concept of what death is, and many understand it more personally through the *physical* death of a loved one. Death, in a larger sense, is a major concern of Scripture, and God's Word provides insights, concepts, and definitions of death far beyond intuitive impressions.

Biblically, the most basic definition of death is separation from God, who is life and the source of all other life. This death occurred immediately, on the very day Adam and Eve sinned just as God said it would:

> And the Lord God commanded the man, saying, Of every tree of the garden thou mayest freely eat [including the tree of life]: But of the tree of the knowledge of good and evil, thou shalt not eat of it: for in the day that thou eatest thereof thou shalt surely die (Gen. 2:16–17).

Even worse, this spiritual death was passed from Adam and Eve to all their children, so human beings are conceived in sin (Ps. 51:5) and *born dead.*

The Scriptures are replete with this message:

- Even when we were dead in sins, hath quickened us together with Christ, (by grace ye are saved) (Eph. 2:5).
- And you, being dead in your sins and the uncircumcision of your flesh, hath he quickened together with him, having forgiven you all trespasses (Col. 2:13).

- For ye are dead, and your life is hid with Christ in God (Col. 3:3).
- For the love of Christ constraineth us; because we thus judge, that if one died for all, then were all dead (2 Cor. 5:14).
- For the wages of sin is death; but the gift of God is eternal life through Jesus Christ our Lord (Rom. 6:23).

The only cure for being born dead in sin is to be born again with new life created through the grace of our Lord Jesus Christ, the author of life! Praise God, the Scriptures are replete also with this blessed message of salvation!

- For as the Father hath life in himself; so hath he given to the Son to have life in himself (John 5:26).
- Jesus said unto her, I am the resurrection, and the life: he that believeth in me, though he were dead, yet shall he live (John 11:25).
- Jesus saith unto him, I am the way, the truth, and the life: no man cometh unto the Father, but by me (John 14:6).
- For God so loved the world, that he gave his only begotten Son, that whosoever believeth in him should not perish, but have everlasting life (John 3:16).

Spiritual death is everlasting — unless it is replaced with everlasting life by new birth in Christ. It is only through the loving sacrifice of the Savior that believers escape the "second death." The first spiritual death occurred with Adam's sin and passed to all mankind. The second death is hell. The second spiritual death is not the cessation of being and personal consciousness; it is everlasting torment where, in Jesus now seldom-quoted words, "there shall be weeping and gnashing of teeth" (Matt. 22:13) and the "worm dieth not" (Mark 9:44).

The horrific thought of sinners in the hands of a justly angry God should drive us into the loving arms of Jesus, who alone can close the separation between God and mankind and restore us to life — rich, abundant, and eternal in heaven with Him!

Physical Death Is the Result of God's Judgment

Most unfortunately, most people are much more concerned with physical death than with the much more important eternal consequences of spiritual death. Physical death is a process of deterioration, a continuing loss of biological order and information that culminates in the triumph of chemistry over biology as the once living body returns to the dust from which it was made.

> In the sweat of thy face shalt thou eat bread, till thou return unto the ground; for out of it wast thou taken: for dust thou art, and unto dust shalt thou return (Gen. 3:19).

The process of dying by which people finally die took 930 years for Adam, 969 for Methuselah (the record holder), and 950 for Noah. (In the Bible, unlike the writings of man's religions, great age was not ascribed as a reward for great faith: the most faithful of the pre-flood patriarchs, Enoch, was taken from earth to heaven as his reward at the tender young age of 365. The Bible's reward is not long life on earth; it is eternal life and a restored relationship with man's Creator.) The Bible goes on to record an accelerating rate of dying after the Flood, resulting in ages in the 800s, 600s, 400s, and 200s until life span settled into the 70–80 year average we have today. Scientists once considered the great ages of the patriarchs an obvious myth, but science has recently done a complete about face. The body seems designed to process food to continually repair itself; the scientific mystery today is not how did the patriarchs live so long, but why do we die so young? Those who take God's Word literally are rejoicing that science has finally caught up and discovered that the Bible has been right all along.

What Is Life?

One might think physical death could be defined most simply as the loss of life — but that requires a definition of life.

Again, people have an intuitive idea of what life is, but the Bible — which is the blessed record of the ultimate triumph of life over death — provides insights, concepts, and definitions of life that go far beyond our intuitive impressions and the present level of scientific knowledge.

Biologists nowadays can define life as an ordered system in which a series of nucleotide bases (in DNA and/or RNA) instruct both the alignment of amino acids to make specific proteins (for structure and function) and the replication of the original base series (for reproduction). That definition can be applied to human beings, animals, plants, microbes, and even viruses. The biblical definition of life is far more restrictive.

In Genesis 1, *ba-ra'* is used for creation *ex nihilo* (from nothing) the creation of something brand new that was not present before, something not just made by rearrangement of previously existing material. The first use of *ba-ra'* is for the *ex nihilo* creation of mass energy at the beginning of time on day 1. Its second use is on day 5, and it refers to the creation of life in the swimming and flying creatures.

Day 5 was the day that God created biblical life and the verb *ba-ra'* appears for the second time in the account of day 5. God brought things into existence by His spoken word on the other days as well, but God specifically uses "create" (*ba-ra'*) to describe what He did when life and creatures are brought into existence. Note that when God brings the creatures into existence, He calls them living (*chayah*) and identifies them as breathers (*nephesh*) that move (*ramas*).

The day 5 creatures *have life!* An expanded translation of Genesis 1:20–23 could well be paraphrased like this:

> God said: "Waters, wiggle with swarms of *nephesh chayah* (breathing life)! Flying things, cover the face of the heaven over the earth!" So, God created great *tanniyn* (monsters, dragons — huge things) and *chayah nephesh* (life-breathing) gliders in the waters that swarmed after their kind and flapping fowl after their kind. And God saw good! Then God blessed them and said: "Bear fruit

and increase. Fill the water in the seas. Fowl, increase in the earth." The dusk and the daybreak were the fifth day.

God's commentary (the good that God saw) is focused on the living things that He has just created. It should not come as a surprise that God is pleased with life. He is life!

Do Plants Have Biblical Life?

Those familiar with the order of God's creative acts in Genesis 1 may have begun wondering by now. What about plants? Plants were created on day 3, but biblical "life" was not created until day 5. Does that mean plants are not alive? Precisely. Plants are replicating systems based on the DNA/protein relationship and do deserve the attention of biologists, but plants do not have biblical life.

The creatures of day 5 were living, breathing, and moving. Given the very specific word selections that the Creator chose to use when describing the day 5 animals, a strong contrast becomes apparent between the creatures of day 5 and the replicating systems of the earth that He orders to sprout on day 3. The earth was to sprout *(dasha)* grass, the herb was to yield *(zara')* seed, and the fruit trees were to make *('asah)* fruit. There was absolutely no hint, when God ordered the earth to bring forth *(yatsa')* its products on day 3, that these elemental foodstuffs (Gen. 1:29) were alive or had the distinction of being called living creatures.

Sometimes one hears a question that comes in a form like this: "You say there was no death before Adam's sin, yet Adam and Eve were given plants to eat. Wouldn't a carrot die if you ate it?" Such a question ignores much of Scripture and science.

Scripturally, plants cannot die because they do not have biblical life *(chayah nephesh)*. God designed green plants to be "good for food" (Gen. 2:9); they are meant to be eaten, and do not have the ability to object to it. To demonstrate the difference between plants and animal life, take a bite from an apple and compare its response to the reaction you get from biting the leg of a dog or cat! The scriptural emphasis on no death before Adam's sin applies only to human life and conscious animal life, because both have *chayah nephesh*. Plants may be uprooted and eaten whole without violating the principle of no death before Adam's sin, because they have no biblical life to lose.

Scientifically speaking, plants — unlike animals — often benefit greatly from being eaten. They were designed as food, and God used that to aid in their growth and propagation. Grasses that are grazed or mowed, and plants that are browsed or pruned regularly grow hardier than those not so cropped. God created plants "pleasant to the sight" (and tasty!), as if to encourage people and animals to eat them — and, if they could be, the plants would be grateful. The seeds of fruits eaten by animals often pass through undigested and later get deposited in a new environment with a bit of fertilizer to help them get started. The calvaria trees in the island of Mauritius were unable to reproduce after the dodo's extinction because only the gizzard of that bird was powerful enough to crack the seed coat sufficiently to allow germination.

The eating of plants in the world God called very good does *not* violate the fundamental biblical teaching of no death before Adam's sin.

Plants, however, might have been used by God to explain the concept of death in His Garden conversations with Adam and Eve. Although not biblically alive, plants are complex and ordered biologically replicating systems. An apple left uneaten on Eden's ground would decay, illustrating the progressive loss of order and information that would (after Eden) also accompany human and animal death.

Creation Is Subject to the Bondage of Decay

Some might object that "decay" would not occur until after Eden, after the creation was subjected to a "bondage of decay" or corruption. Consider that "decay," like so many words, has more than one meaning. The "decay" of uneaten fruit or of leaves falling in autumn (seasons were established on creation day 4) would be part of the biogeochemical recycling system that God could easily call very good. In contrast, "decay" can also refer to the process of dying, the deterioration of order and information with time. That kind of decay, the death principle, became a part of our world only after Eden, when the whole cosmos was brought under a "bondage of corruption" or decay.

The *universal principle of aging and death*, called the "*bondage of corruption*" in biblical language (Rom. 8:21), is called the second law of thermodynamics in scientific language. One of the most thoroughly documented and most broadly applied laws in all of science, the second law describes *change through time* in an isolated system left to itself and the vagaries of time and chance: all such systems spontaneously and naturally lose useful energy, order, information — or any two or all three of those! The second law is sometimes called *"Time's Arrow,"* and the arrow points DOWN!

Notice that there are two views of *"change through time."* *Evolutionists* like to define evolution seductively as "change through time" (after all, who can object to that?); but they believe that this naturalistic, godless change through time ultimately yields an upward progressive "creation." All the branches of science tell us exactly the opposite: naturalistic, after Eden change through time is ultimately a *downward regressive corruption*!

Do not misunderstand; the second law *does* allow an *increase* in energy, order, and/or information — but IF AND ONLY IF there is an "outside source of greater energy, order, and/or information." For example, a seedling can grow into a tree, because it has an outside useful source (the sun), an exquisitely multi-faceted ordered system to harness that energy (the green plant cell's chloroplast), and coordinated sets of information programmed into the DNA of both the plant cell's nucleus and the chloroplasts! Remove the light, and the seedling dies. Put it in the sunshine but destroy its energy-harnessing chloroplasts, and the seedling dies. When all three — energy, order, and information — are properly in place, the seedling grows into a tree that can produce thousands of other seeds and seedlings like itself!

The sun that provides the energy the seedling harnesses, however, is dissipating itself. Every second, 4.5 million tons of the sun are scattered irretrievably into space; the sun is burning out! (Do not worry, though; God created the sun so huge that it could lose useful energy and order at that stunning rate while still supplying energy for life on earth all the way up to Christ's return).

These two examples present the ultimate problem reflected in the second law. One system can gain useful energy and/or order IF AND ONLY IF another system loses *more* useful energy and/or order than the first system gains. According to "Time's Arrow," the *net* change through time is *loss* of useful energy and/or order. As in the game called "gossip" (in which a story is whispered around a circle), information, left to the natural influences of time and chance, usually becomes more garbled through time. In spite of absolutely incredible cellular mechanisms for proofreading and error correction, the genetic information programmed into DNA also deteriorates with time in our post-Eden world. God alone can transfer information (and useful energy and order) without loss. Praise God, He created His image-bearers with sufficient information and a highly ordered nervous system so that, with a lot of energy applied to study and discovery, mankind can process a bit more information each generation!

The second law is not inherently evil of itself; it merely reflects the direction in which events flow through time. Water flowing downhill, the life-energizing (NOT life-giving) dissipation of the sun, and the scent of fresh flowers spreading through a room are all examples of the second law in action. With God's infinite supply of useful energy, order, and information operating in His perfectly designed universe, the second law could play a directive role in God's very good creation, its negative effects only manifest after the ground (the elemental substances of the universe) was cursed following Adam's sin.

For living things, including human beings (and for replicating systems like plants), the most devastating effect of the second law after Eden is the spontaneous deterioration and loss of genetic information in DNA. These random changes in genes are called *mutations*. Incredibly, evolutionists call mutations "the raw material for evolution" and believe the net effect of mutations over time, culled by struggle and death (natural selection), is the continuous origin of "new and improved" species. In direct opposition to the evolutionists' baseless belief, scientists observe that the net effect of mutations over time (slowed by natural selection) is the continuous origin of disease organisms and defects. If the Bible taught evolution, scientists would find it easy to disprove it! Geneticists call the effects of mutations "genetic burden" or "genetic load" to convey the fact that mutations produce a genetic decay that drags down the quality of a species.

Time makes the effects of genetic burden worse and worse. The human population, for example, has already accumulated over 4,500 harmful mutations. It has been suggested that married couples should soon be required to obtain an additional license that could be obtained only after they passed a test screening them for genetic defects. Some evolutionists are even saying species may go extinct because of accumulating mutational load within an average of 5 million years, a mere "blink of the eye" in their time frame.

Some mutations are known to bring early death, and they may have contributed to a declining life span in both man and animals after Eden, especially after the Flood. As discussed in chapter 6, mutations may have disrupted both territorial instincts and digestive processes leading to dietary changes, predatory behavior, and population imbalances. The Bible specifically cites the production of thorns and thistles in plants after Eden and implies the overgrowth of weeds, changing mankind's pleasure at dressing and keeping the Garden into the toilsome eking out of existence by the sweat of the brow until finally returning to dust (Gen. 3:18–19). The earth's crust is full of fossils that testify to the horrors of struggle and death and of God's judgment.

The physical side of creation, as well, is not immune from the bondage of decay. Some elements in the cursed ground even decompose radioactively, perhaps foreshadowing the final end of this cosmos when "the elements melt with fervent heat" (2 Pet. 3:10). On the positive side, radioactive deteriorating should also remind us that it is only in Christ that "all things consist" (Col. 1:17).

Even the heavens are disintegrating. Comets deteriorate with each pass around the sun. Craters pock mark the solar systems. Stars age; some explode. Praise God, even the heavens will be made new at Christ's return.

Christian compromisers may want to take the "bondage of corruption" allegorically, but living things, earth, and the universe manifest its effects very literally!

It is ironic that those who want to change God's Word to conform to the pronouncements of some scientists, must ignore true science in order to maintain respectability among evolutionists who also must ignore the demonstrated downward effects of the second law to maintain their faith in the upwardly progressive "creation"! If the Bible did not teach a bondage of corruption and curse on the ground, scientists would have reason to question the knowledge of its author.

As it is, however, what we see in God's world (science) makes sense in the light of God's Word — the whole gospel message from God's perfect creation, to the corruption and catastrophe brought on by mankind's sin to the blessed final restoration of all things in Christ!

These are difficult concepts to evaluate, but they are critically important to the gospel message of the Scriptures. Perhaps a review of what has been discussed and an application of the principles is in order.

The Creator Must Now Conquer Death

God executed a sentence on His heretofore good creation that introduced a punishment on it all. After Adam sinned, God pronounced a curse on the ground. The awful consequences of rebellion would now begin to bear their fruit in the realm of men. They had been granted freedom and authority; now they would reap sorrow and worry. They had been given a Garden to dress; now they would sweat for their harvest. They had been given life; now they were dead. The magnificent sculpture of God's image with its potential and privilege of an eternal youth would now slowly decay and return to the dust from which it was manufactured. Every aspect of their life had changed. Where good proliferated, evil now dominated. Where life flourished, death now reigned (Rom. 5:17).

Some have suggested that all living things were originally designed by God to die: that over the millions of years in which animal and pre-human life was developing, death played a perfectly natural role in creation. Some have taught that the death with which God threatened Adam was a special kind of death that applied only to humans. The written words of God do not teach this. *Death is, in its most succinct form*, separation from the life of the Creator. *Death has its fruit physically*, when the body decays back to the dust of its origin. Death for a human being is, however, much more than the cessation of activity. Death is a disconnection, a disharmony, a dislocation from the source. Death severs us from God.

The Bible says that death is an intrusion — a punishment for the creatures' rebellion against the Creator. The Bible says that there will be a restoration — a reconciliation of all things — and that that restoration will eliminate death. The Bible also says that death must be defeated by the Creator overcoming death.

The Creator pronounced the sentence of death (Gen. 3).

The Creator will overcome death (1 Cor. 15).

The Creator has life in himself (John 1, 8, 11).

The Creator must give His life to give us life (John 10).

The Creator grants eternal life to all who believe His words (John 12).

Why would people want to deny the Creator's words? Could it be that they do not believe that the omnipotent Creator of the Bible really exists? Could it be that they want to believe that the created thing is as good as the Creator? Could it be that they do not believe in the goodness of the Creator but in the pleasure of evil or praises of men? If the Creator does not exist, if what we see and experience in this life is all that exists, then where is the hope? In Christ who conquers death for us and the whole creation!

- Wherefore, as by one man sin entered into the world, and death by sin; and so death passed upon all men, for that all have sinned (Rom. 5:12).
- Therefore as by the offence of one judgment came upon all men to condemnation (Rom. 5:18).
- Who his own self bare our sins in his own body on the tree, that we, being dead to sins, should live unto righteousness: by whose stripes ye were healed (1 Pet. 2:24).
- Verily, verily, I say unto you, He that heareth my word, and believeth on him that sent me, hath everlasting life, and shall not come into condemnation; but is passed from death unto life (John 5:24).
- Being born again, not of corruptible seed, but of incorruptible, by the word of God, which liveth and abideth for ever (1 Pet. 1:23).

Who shall deliver me from the body of this death? (Rom. 7:24).

Endnotes

1 Lars Ulrich, quoted in Perspectives, *Newsweek*, June 9, 2003, p. 23.

Chapter 10

Being Overflowed with Water

In nearly every case, for both big extinctions and more modest ones, we have bewilderingly little idea of what the cause was.[1]

— Bill Bryson in *A Short History of Nearly Everything*

Nothing seems to rouse intellectual resistance — and emotional reaction — more than the suggestion that the universe is young. The mantra "millions of years ago" has become so fixed in the academic mind that many can hardly conceive of a young earth. Western education is so saturated with "oldness" that every discipline promotes a long story of origins. The scientist is no longer the only prophet of evolution, but has been joined by the professors of sociology, politics, art, history, and math. In every venue from the Discovery Channel to Disneyland, the assumption is upheld that science has proven vast ages of the past.

All who teach the naturalistic development of life do so with the absolute belief that it *requires* long ages. That requirement is precisely the point. If evolution is the process by which things came to be, then long ages are *absolutely necessary* for evolution to take place. For this reason, proponents of evolution do not accept the idea of a young earth.

Now, why is that?

Dr. George Wald authored an important book describing the processes that would be necessary to bring life into existence.

Though he admitted the serious difficulties involved with the huge leap from unrelated non-living chemicals to living organisms, he insisted that such an event must have happened. Much has been added to his ideas over the years, but his observation about the necessity of long ages remains quite perceptive.

> The important point is that since the origin of life belongs in the category of at-least-once phenomena, time is on its side. However improbable we regard this event . . . given enough time it will almost certainly happen at least once. . . .
>
> Time is in fact the hero of the plot. The time with which we have to deal is of the order of two billion years. What we regard as impossible on the basis of human experience is meaningless here. Given so much time, the "impossible" becomes possible, the possible probable, and the probable virtually certain. One has only to wait: time itself performs the miracles.[2]

Without the miracle of long ages, human experience would reject the idea that random naturalistic events could produce any order — let alone the wonder and awe of our universe. Unimaginable ages become the rationale for unthinkable processes. *Anything* can happen if there is enough time for *things* to happen. Twenty-five years after Dr. Wald made public his famous assertion on the necessity of long ages, Carl Sagan, in his famous book *Cosmos*, reiterates the critical role of the ages:

> The secrets of evolution are death and time — the deaths of enormous numbers of life forms that were imperfectly adapted to the environment; and time for a long succession of small mutations that were *by accident* adaptive, time for the slow accumulation of patterns of favorable mutations.[3]

Evolutionary thinking has gone through an evolution of its own over the decades since Wald and Sagan wrote their books. Darwin's concept that natural selection slowly "upgraded" life over millions of years has presented such difficulties for paleontologists that a whole new school called *punctuated equilibrium* has arisen to explain the abrupt appearance in the fossil record of the different species of animals. This theory, made popular mainly by Stephen J. Gould of Harvard, suggests that new species arise by radical genomic rearrangements and/or "super mutations" in regulatory genes. The resulting dramatic changes happen too completely and too rapidly to be preserved in the geologic record. These large and sudden changes burst into the fossil sequence, punctuating long periods of equilibrium or of "stasis," when few or no changes were occurring.

Long ages are still involved!

Concerning the vast numbers and varieties of complex invertebrates in the Cambrian fossil beds across the world, Gould writes: "So even the most cautious opinion holds that 500 million subsequent years of opportunity have not expanded the Cambrian range, achieved in just five million years. The Cambrian explosion was the most remarkable and puzzling event in the history of life."[4] From Gould's viewpoint, although an amazing variety of forms appeared in a very short evolutionary time, it still required five million years to produce this so-called remarkable achievement even though almost nothing happened in the subsequent 500 million years!

Without long ages, macro-evolution of any type is just not believable.

Geologic Strata and Fossils Are Used as Proof for Long Ages

Ask the common man how he knows that earth is old, and he will likely point to the rocks and the fossils. Earth scientists study more hard data than do the more theoretical astronomers and astrophysicists. Geological exploration has been responsible for uncovering stores of fossil fuels, and the mining sciences have delved deep into the earth to search out its riches. Much has been laid bare and subsequently evaluated. For nearly 200 years, geology — at least the geology of Charles Lyell and his followers — has been attaching ages to the geological column and has been using those ages as proof for evolution.

The rocks and fossils in the geologic column have become the "bible" of evolutionary thought. They are claimed to be hard evidence for the long ages of naturalistic development, and they are supplemented by the more recent development of radiometric dating. Consider these bold (but baseless) beliefs:

- Although the comparative study of living animals and plants may give very convincing circumstantial evidence, fossils provide the only historical, documentary evidence that life has evolved from simpler to more and more complex forms. (Carl O. Dunbar)[5]

- Fortunately there is a science which is able to observe the progress of evolution through the history of our earth. Geology traces the rocky strata of our earth, deposited one upon another in the past geological epochs through hundreds of millions of years, and finds out their order and timing and reveals organisms which lived in all these periods. Paleontology, which studies the fossil remains, is thus enabled to present organic evolution as a visible fact. . . . (Richard Goldschmidt)[6]

Although both of the above were written several decades ago, the evidence for evolution is still thought to reside in the rocks and fossils arranged by "index fossils." The 2003 electronic edition of the *Encyclopedia Britannica* defines index fossils as:

> Any animal or plant preserved in the rock record of the earth that is characteristic of a particular span of geologic time or environment. A useful index fossil must be distinctive or easily recognizable, abundant, and have a wide geographic distribution and a short range through time. Index fossils are the basis for defining boundaries in the geologic time scale. . . .[7]

Even though geological science has gravitated toward radiometric dating as the main claim for long ages, the fossil beds are still thought to provide the hard evidence for evolutionary progression. If those fossils (and the rocks which contain them) were deposited by the year-long global flood the Bible describes, then the interpretation of the fossil record must be *very* different. Index fossils, for example, would then mark different *locations* (pre-Flood environmental zones) rather than different *times*.

Genesis Clearly Teaches a Worldwide Flood

The catastrophic energies and devastating events of the year-long disaster described in Genesis left an earth restructured and horribly disfigured — an earth drastically changed in many ways. The rupture of the "fountains of the great deep" began the cataclysm spoken of by Peter (2 Pet. 3:6) during which the world perished. Since, as has been shown, the relatively sparse information in Genesis about the creation week should be accepted as written, certainly the voluminous biblical data on the destruction of "the world that then was" seems to be beyond contention. God devotes portions of four chapters (Genesis 6–9) and over 1,700 words to this unique event; the creation account is half that long. Other portions of Scripture buttress its teachings.

Surely, it is clear from the biblical record that God intended to destroy an entire world population that had become so wicked that "every imagination of the thoughts of [man's] heart was only evil continually" (Gen. 6:5). In seven different passages in Genesis, the Flood's global nature is specifically declared or clearly referred to:

- The earth also was corrupt before God, and the earth was filled with violence. And God looked upon the earth, and, behold, it was corrupt; for all flesh had corrupted his way upon the earth. And God said unto Noah, *The end of all flesh* is come before me; for the earth is filled with violence through them; and, behold, I will destroy them with the earth (Gen. 6:11–13; emphasis added).

- And, behold, I, even I, do bring a flood of waters upon the earth, to destroy *all flesh*, wherein is the breath of life, from under heaven; and *every thing* that is in the earth shall die (Gen. 6:17; emphasis added).

- For yet seven days, and I will cause it to rain upon the earth forty days and forty nights; and *every living substance* that I have made will I destroy from off the face of the earth (Gen. 7:4; emphasis added).

- And *all flesh* died that moved upon the earth, both of fowl, and of cattle, and of beast, and of every creeping thing that creepeth upon the earth, and *every man*: All in whose nostrils was the breath of life, of all that was in the dry land, died. And *every living substance* was destroyed which was upon the face of the ground, both man, and cattle, and the creeping things, and the fowl of the heaven; and they were destroyed from the earth: and Noah only remained alive, and they that were with him in the ark (Gen. 7:21–23).

Notice the extravagant repetition (something rare in most of Scripture): all flesh . . . all in whose nostrils . . . every living substance. Even examples are given and repeated: fowl, cattle, beast, creeping thing, man; then man, cattle, creeping thing, and fowl! The Lord also repeats His promise never again to send such a Flood!

- And the Lord smelled a sweet savour; and the Lord said in his heart, I will not again curse the ground any more for man's sake; for the imagination of man's heart is evil from his youth; neither will I again smite any more *every thing living*, as I have done (Gen. 8:21; emphasis added).

- And I will establish my covenant with you; neither shall *all flesh* be cut off any more by the waters of a flood; neither shall there any more be a flood to destroy the earth (Gen. 9:11; emphasis added).

- And I will remember my covenant, which is between me and you and every living creature of all flesh; and the waters shall no more become a flood to destroy *all flesh* (Gen. 9:15; emphasis added).

Those passages present a precise set of words and a very specific grammatical construction that clearly identifies the reason for the Flood, the extent of the Flood, and its uniqueness. Again, God appears to have gone to great lengths to ensure that the readers of His revealed Word would completely understand what He intended to do and why He did what He did. If God merely intended to destroy the settlements in the Mesopotamian river valley, He was using grossly exaggerated language. If these words do not mean what they clearly say, then how can we trust any portion of Scripture?

The Bible record, however, speaks of God's judgment on an evil world population — that He executed in such a way that every air-breathing animal in the world would be destroyed! This level of catastrophe could not be local and also remain consistent with the biblical passage. The Bible unmistakably records a worldwide event.

The carefully constructed language of Genesis insists that the volume of water was so great that:

- It increased in depth for at least 40 days (Gen. 7:17).
- It covered all the mountains under the whole heaven (Gen. 7:18–20).
- It was 150 days before the waters began to go down and the ark could sit on the mountains of Ararat (Gen.7:24, 8:4).
- The mountains remained covered for another two and one-half months (Gen. 8:5).
- The water covered the lower land surfaces an additional three and one-half months (Gen. 8:6–14).
- The total flood duration was 371 days, or 53 weeks (Gen. 7:11, 8:14).

That language does not describe a local or a tranquil flood!

Evolutionary Science Cannot Accept the Genesis Account

Most evolutionary geologists and paleontologists simply dismiss the biblical record altogether. These scientists do not attempt to argue with the record — they just reject it. For them, there is no supernatural deity who has created or judged people for their choices. The Bible is merely a collection of ancient stories that have little or no basis in fact. At least the evolutionists' beliefs are consistent with their presuppositions.

Those Christian compromisers, on the other hand, who would deconstruct the biblical record to make it mean something else must do so in spite of all the biblical evidence to the contrary. Those who insist that this record of the year-long, mountain-covering flood is something other than what the Bible states it is, do so because such an event would eradicate evidence for the long geological ages required for evolution. They believe in a naturalistic explanation for the worldwide deposits of sedimentary rock and trillions of fossilized dead creatures. They oppose the words of the text and try to manufacture a compromise that will satisfy both the biblical language and the scientific establishment.

They fail both scripturally and scientifically.

If the Flood as recorded in Genesis actually occurred, the entire surface of the earth would show the record of the colossal scouring and restructuring. Fountains of the great deep exploded, fracturing the earth's crust and unleashing torrents of pressurized water and huge flows of magma from deep inside the earth. Those torrents would generate tsunamis against the continents, pulverizing and inundating everything in their paths. Huge turbidity currents and underwater mudslides (debris flows) would have swept sediments across the continents.

The Bible says that torrential rain poured continuously for 40 days. Enormous waves would have added to the mix of destruction, leaving nothing untouched. Those who escaped the explosions of the fountains would drown in the floodwaters — many perhaps being sucked down in the countless whirlpools generated by the violent waves and underwater currents. Some people may have clung to tossing debris for a few long moments, but they would eventually have been torn from their support like a dead leaf in a quick autumn breeze. Nothing on land would survive.

As mountains later uplifted, the land surface was re-shaped and gorges formed (Ps. 104:6–9). The whole of the earth was eroded, and sediments were redeposited while the waters crashed back and forth unabated (Gen. 7:24 and 8:3). Everything that lived on the land and in the air was killed (Gen. 7:23). Billions upon billions of life forms were buried under hundreds and thousands of feet of mud and debris. Currents and hydraulic turmoil separated and segregated the debris into layer upon layer of sedimentary deposits, often containing mangled and dismembered plant and animal remains.

While representatives of sea life survived, countless billions of water creatures would have been buried as vast amounts of land sediment crashed into the sea and sea sediments swept onto the land. Bottom dwellers were virtually defenseless, of course, and became engulfed by the tons of mud sloshing about in their environment. Others were swept together in mounds of biologic stew and ground into a sour organic mash. Swarms of fish were instantly buried — some in the act of swallowing their meals. Mound upon mound of living things were crushed and buried.

Creatures great and small were engulfed by the torrents and roiled together in vast maelstroms that would swirl for weeks. Those not pulverized by the gigantic forces were entombed in the mud and clay and sand and lime of the turbid mix. Humanity was obliterated. Some may have escaped the early stages of the catastrophe only to have been drowned later. They would eventually decay or be devoured by scavengers. A few, perhaps, were swept into a sedimentary tomb and fossilized, to be eventually discovered in the years to come.

Nothing would ever be the same!

The wonder of the good creation, more evident between Fall and Flood than today, was destroyed. Only eight souls (1 Pet. 3:20) accepted the provision of salvation Noah preached for 120 years. These eight people and two of each kind of dry land animal (seven of the clean kinds), several thousand total, God preserved on the ark (Gen. 8:17). Many sea creatures survived in the open water, but many others were included in the scarred and pock-marked sediments that entombed the results of God's wrath.

If the Genesis Flood Is True, What Should We Expect To Find?

The description above was drawn from the pages of Scripture; yet it is compatible with geological observations. If such an event did indeed take place as the Bible teaches, then what should we (on this side of the cataclysm) expect to find as evidence?

- *Bottom-dwelling marine life in every conceivable environment on the planet:* The flood of Noah would have carried and deposited clams, snails, starfish, trilobites, corals, sponges, and all the shelled sea creatures with a high fossilization potential. Their fossils are found everywhere — on mountaintops, in desert valleys, in canyons, and beneath rolling plains. The *worldwide*, year-long, mountain-submerging Flood leads us to expect to find just what we do find!
- *Preservation of every kind of animal, in every conceivable condition — some whole, some broken, mangled, disarticulated, and lumped together as well as some separated by size and type — distributed over the entire surface of the earth:* We would expect that the vast majority of these creatures would give evidence of catastrophic and rapid burial with lithification of fossil deposits. We would expect to find just what we do find!
- *Many large graveyards of fossil deposits with creatures of every type and from diverse environments, violently killed, washed together, buried together, and fossilized rapidly:* Frequent mixing of various types of animals would also occur. We would expect to find just what we do find!
- *Throughout the world and in all types of deposits, preserved "soft" parts, ephemeral markings, and tracks that*

could only be preserved under the most rapid and unique burial conditions — conditions that rapidly deteriorate when exposed to erosion: We would expect to find just what we do find!

- *The distinctive presence of every kind of animal, with clear differences between the types:* The God who brought the Flood, was also the One who created the animals. He set the boundaries, or reproductive limits, between the kinds. The burial ground would hold the remains of the original kinds. They would be distinct and different. We would expect to find just what we do find!
- *Common structural features (rifts, faults, folds, thrusts, dikes, and similar features) everywhere in all types of deposits with many areas bearing the imprint of vast energies shaping the rocks during stages prior to their solidification:* We would expect to find just what we do find!
- *Worldwide evidence of recent bodies of water existing in desert areas, worldwide occurrences of raised shore lines and river terraces, valleys much too large for the present rivers and streams, clear traces of rapid rise in sea levels:* If the flood of Genesis occurred, we would expect to find just what we do find!

This Is the Message from Scripture and the Evidence Left Behind

- The Bible teaches a worldwide Flood.
- The Creator was enraged by the rebellion of His creatures.
- The Flood was designed by God to destroy all air-breathing life.
- The destruction was complete and total and forever changed the earth.

- The grace of the Creator preserved life on the earth through the ark.
- The God of judgment made a covenant of conservation with all life.
- The present earth bears the worldwide marks of that global flood.

The geological and paleontological evidence is exactly what one would expect to find as the products of the flood of Genesis. Those who deny the Bible record do so either from ignorance or because they have chosen to believe naturalistic and evolutionary (hence, atheistic) science over Scripture. The evolutionist does not accept the biblical record. The Lord Jesus, however, does (Luke 17:26–27).

> Whereby the world that then was, being overflowed with water, perished (2 Pet. 3:6).

Endnotes

1 Bill Bryson, *A Short History of Nearly Everything* (New York: Broadway Books, 2003), p. 344.
2 *The Physics and Chemistry of Life*, "The Origin of Life," by George Wald (New York: Simon and Schuster, 1955), p. 12.
3 Carl Sagan, *Cosmos* (New York: Random House, 1980), p. 30.
4 Stephen J. Gould, "The Evolution of Life on the Earth," *Scientific American*, October 1994, p. 89.
5 Carl O. Dunbar, *Historical Geology*, 2nd ed. (New York: John Wiley & Sons, 1960), p. 47.
6 Richard B. Goldschmidt, "An Introduction to a Popularized Symposium on Evolution," *The Scientific Monthly*, 77, October 1953, 184.
7 Encyclopaedia Britannica Premium Service, s.v. "Index fossil," http://www.britannica.com/eb/article?eu=43223 (accessed October 15, 2003).

Chapter 11

Great Swelling Words

The little Book of Jude contains an intriguing passage that quotes Enoch, a preacher who lived before the time of Noah's flood. Jude used the opportunity to describe the rebellious characteristics of certain men known to him who had rejected God's authority, just like they did in Noah's day.

> Enoch . . . prophesied of these, saying, Behold, the Lord cometh with ten thousands of his saints, to execute judgment upon all, and to convince all that are ungodly among them. . . . These are murmurers, complainers, walking after their own lusts; and their mouth speaketh great swelling words, having men's persons in admiration because of advantage" (Jude 14–16).

Other translations chose less confrontive language: "speak arrogantly" (NAS), "boast about themselves" (NIV), and "loud mouth boasters" (RSV). All of these renderings point out that Enoch was reproving people who would use pompous and arrogant language to awe the audience with complex verbal intricacies — intending to control others with their rhetoric.

Those who oppose Scripture have used this technique to deceive and manipulate men. An important educational degree, for instance, can be used as a weapon to silence any critic who would dare question the authority of the expert in a given field. With the sweep of an academic hand, those without the proper credentials are dismissed or disdained. Reconstruction of language has become an all too common manipulative tool. The academic, judicial, and political systems have fashioned the re-definition of terms into a scholarly methodology, "spoiling" (Col. 2:8) Christians by this subtle tactic.

It is important to expose the logic and persuasive skills used by those who would try to intimidate and awe the audience rather than humbly teach the sincere student. This part examines their impact and attempts to expose their arrogant techniques which are undermining the authority of the Word of God.

It is time for both Christian leaders and Christian laymen to be Berean (Acts 17:11). Leaders need to follow Paul's example, teaching plainly, bringing honor to God and not to themselves. Laymen need to be prepared, through knowledge of God's Word, to challenge those who are overly wise in their own eyes.

Chapter 12

Hermeneutical Gymnastics

I don't feel I have to justify myself to anybody but myself.[1]

— U.S. District Judge
Jack B. Weinstein

In the late 1990s, President Bill Clinton, entangled in a scandal of his own making, gave the world one of the best examples of language reconstruction. He had betrayed a trust with one of his office employees and had behaved improperly with her. As the events unfolded before the public eye, the president made various statements that openly denied any misbehavior. However, a cadre of legal experts was convened to investigate the mounting evidence that disgraceful conduct had indeed been committed actually on several occasions and with more than one employee.

During the course of the investigation, depositions were taken by the parties concerned. Due to the stature of the presidency, video cameras were present for most of them. The young woman at the center of the controversy issued an affidavit, part of which said, "There is absolutely no sex of any kind in any manner, shape or form" between the president and herself.[2] Later, during a lengthy grand jury hearing, the statement was read to the president and he was asked, simply, if the statement was true. Marking one of the lowest moments in the American presidency, Mr. Clinton responded, "It depends upon what the meaning of the word 'is,' is."[3]

In spite of the world's astonishment, a few highly qualified and very intelligent men and women began to claim that the president was not to be blamed, building their case on extended and reconstructed definitions of "is" and "alone" and "cause" and "sexual relations." In doing so, they changed the obvious meaning of the clear terminology in such a way that "black" turned into "white." The sad part of this true story is that these subtle arguments succeeded in controlling the opinions of a large part of the world's population!

The Scripture sternly warns those who would call evil good and good evil, thereby, twisting the words of Scripture and the themes of God for their own ends:

> Woe unto them that call evil good, and good evil; that put darkness for light, and light for darkness; that put bitter for sweet, and sweet for bitter! Woe unto them that are wise in their own eyes, and prudent in their own sight! . . . . Therefore as the fire devoureth the stubble, and the flame consumeth the chaff, so their root shall be as rottenness, and their blossom shall go up as dust: because they have cast away the law of the Lord of hosts, and despised the word of the Holy One of Israel (Isa. 5:20–24).

Deconstruction of Scripture Is Old News

Changing the words of Scripture is nothing new. For centuries, some Bible scholars have attempted to "interpret" the words of God for their own ends. Origen, called by some the "father" of allegorical interpretation, lived and taught during the early 200s at a school in Alexandria, Egypt. Essentially, he insisted that the real meaning of Scripture was not in the historical narrative but in some spiritual truth that could be gleaned only by searching after its hidden sense.

Origen coined 40 terms for this "heavenly sense" — all dependent in one way or another upon finding the "true" meaning behind the actual words. He was particularly driven to accommodate the science of his day. The sophisticated and intellectual world of imported Greek culture was at its zenith in Egypt during the first and second centuries, and Origen was determined to conform the words of Scripture to the understanding of the day. One writer describes him this way:

> His mind slips incessantly away from the real scenes and events recorded in Scripture, to the ideal region where he conceives that the truths reside which these prefigure. Scripture is to him not a record of actual occurrences which took place as they are narrated, but a storehouse of types of heavenly things, which alone are real. He scoffs at the notion that historical facts should be regarded as the chief outcome of a Scripture narrative (John, book x.15-17, p. 389-394) . . . but that the literal meaning of the passages must be altogether disregarded and their true purport looked for, not in the things of history, but in the things of the Spirit.[4]

Not much has changed over the centuries. Scholars still seem to be drawn to the "hidden meanings" of Bible words rather than to the words themselves. In some arenas, theology has become a human "science" that studies men's words rather than God's Word and teaches its adherents the processes of a certain hermeneutic, which will set their school of thought apart from others. Sadly, all such schools place the filter of their own hermeneutic over the words of Scripture. Some filters are more opaque than others, but all of them tend to obscure the simple revelation of God with personal agendas.

Faithful pastors and theologians have a different agenda. While there can be only one correct understanding, there are many applications of the Bible passages. Applying the eternal principles and truths of the words of Scripture to the circumstances of human life is both necessary and honorable. That role is assigned, in the Scripture, to the pastor and Bible teacher.

No one has the right to change the words of God to suit his idea of what it *should* mean. The most onerous of "interpretations" is that which openly subverts the clear and precise words of God with the opinions and ideas of man. The Pharisees' subversion is exactly what the Lord Jesus so angrily denounced (Matt. 23). They had nullified the words of God by their traditions. They had overridden the books of Moses with the writings of the scribes. They had twisted the law of God into the endless and ridiculous rules of men.

Today, the Pharisees' technique would be called "reconstruction" or "deconstruction." Some seminaries would call the process "interpretation." Whatever the name, the practice is still the same. Some authority, outside of the author of Scripture, is exalted as *the* authority and looked to as the only qualified source for proper interpretation of the words. In a cult, that authority is the cult leader. For some, the authority may be a special "bible" or "key" to the Scripture. Sometimes it is a doctrinal creed or church canon. Intellectuals exalt logic or "science," mystics exalt extra-natural forces, followers exalt testimonials, and crowds exalt emotion or experience. In each case, someone or something supersedes (that is the point) the authority of God's Word.

Common Sense Is Common Sense

Most Christians would be surprised at the volumes of words that have been generated in the discussion of one word. These "great swelling words" are symptomatic of the effort required to explain away what God has said. A basic principle of logic in biblical exposition is: "If the plain sense makes common sense, seek no other sense." Quite a number of variations on this theme exist among the sayings of common experience. One of the most often used is the "KISS Formula" (Keep It Simple, Stupid). The point is always the same. The further one diverges from the truth, the more explanation and obfuscation is necessary to cover the error.

Please make this biblical warning your constant guard: "But I fear, lest by any means, as the serpent beguiled Eve through his subtilty, so your minds should be corrupted from the *simplicity that is in Christ*" (2 Cor. 11:3; emphasis added).

Truth Brings Clarity; Error Breeds Confusion

Jesus spoke often of the liberty that truth will bring to man's heart, and He insisted that God was careful to ensure that we would be able to understand what truth was.

- And ye shall know the truth, and the truth shall make you free. . . . If the Son therefore shall make you free, ye shall be free indeed (John 8:32–36).
- Jesus saith unto him, I am the way, the truth, and the life: no man cometh unto the Father, but by me (John 14:6).
- For I have not spoken of myself; but the Father which sent me, he gave me a commandment, what I should say, and what I should speak. And I know that his commandment is life everlasting: whatsoever I speak therefore, even as the Father said unto me, so I speak (John 12:49–50).
- Howbeit when he, the Spirit of truth, is come, he will guide you into all truth: for he shall not speak of himself; but whatsoever he shall hear, that shall he speak: and he will shew you things to come (John 16:13).
- Sanctify them through thy truth: thy word is truth (John 17:17).

How much more emphatically could this principle be expressed? Our Lord was very precise and very passionate about truth. Those who have chosen to reject Christ's deity often use consistent logical reasoning to reject or question His teaching. Those scholars, however, who claim to believe in the deity of Jesus Christ — yet want to distort what He said — are very inconsistent (to say the least). If these scholars claim to believe in the omniscience of Jesus Christ (an attribute integral to biblical teaching about God), then they should not impose their ideas about what God "really meant" on the words that God uses to teach His truth.

God makes a wonderful promise to liberally grant wisdom to us when we ask Him for it (James 1:5–8). The New Testament word for "wisdom" is the Greek word *sophia* which emphasizes the so-called common sense of practicality and effectiveness. *Sophia* is the kind of knowledge that is both easy to use and easy to apply. God's *sophia* clarifies and empowers.

- Because that which may be known of God is manifest in them; for God hath shewed it unto them. For the invisible things . . . are clearly seen, being understood by the things that are made. . . . Professing themselves to be wise, they became fools, And changed the glory of the uncorruptible God into an image made like to corruptible man. . . . Who changed the truth of God into a lie, and worshipped and served the creature more than the Creator, who is blessed for ever. Amen (Rom. 1:19–25).
- Unto all riches of the full assurance of understanding, to the acknowledgement of the mystery of God, and of the Father, and of Christ; In whom are hid all the treasures of wisdom and knowledge (Col. 2:2–3).
- Walk in wisdom toward them that are without, redeeming the time. Let your speech be alway with grace, seasoned with salt, that ye may know how ye ought to answer every man (Col. 4:5–6).

Error always includes just enough truth to disguise its effort to distort, and it always requires additional "double talk" to subvert what God has revealed. Remember the biblical declaration: "God is light, and in him is no darkness at all" (1 John 1:5). Every effort to deceive is couched in a barrage of words that attempt to "explain" or "interpret" truth in a "different light."

- For such are false apostles, deceitful workers, transforming themselves into the apostles of Christ. And no marvel; for Satan himself is transformed into an angel of light. Therefore it is no great thing if his ministers also be transformed as the ministers of righteousness; whose end shall be according to their works (2 Cor. 11:13–15).

- But I fear, lest by any means, as the serpent beguiled Eve through his subtilty, so your minds should be corrupted from the simplicity that is in Christ. For if he that cometh preacheth another Jesus, whom we have not preached, or if ye receive another spirit, which ye have not received, or another gospel, which ye have not accepted, ye might well bear with him (2 Cor. 11:3–4).
- I marvel that ye are so soon removed from him that called you into the grace of Christ unto another gospel: Which is not another; but there be some that trouble you, and would pervert the gospel of Christ. But though we, or an angel from heaven, preach any other gospel unto you than that which we have preached unto you, let him be accursed (Gal. 1:6–8).

Throughout Scripture, the term "light" applies to truth. God ordered a separation between light and darkness when He created the universe. It was that distinction that God called good on the first day, and it is that distinction that sets God apart from every other being in the universe (1 John 1:5). That created condition of absolute contrast is applied by God to our lifestyle. We are to be "day-like" and not "dark-like."

- But ye, brethren, are not in darkness, that that day should overtake you as a thief. Ye are all the children of light, and the children of the day: we are not of the night, nor of darkness (1 Thess. 5:4–5).
- And this is the condemnation, that light is come into the world, and men loved darkness rather than light, because their deeds were evil. For every one that doeth evil hateth the light, neither cometh to the light, lest his deeds should be reproved. But he that doeth truth

cometh to the light, that his deeds may be made manifest, that they are wrought in God (John 3:19–21).

In the Beginning Was the Word . . .

Words mean a great deal to God, and verbal communication between God and His image-bearers set mankind dramatically apart from God's other creative works. The Creator identifies himself as the Word. The apostle John builds the foundation for accepting Jesus' words and their eternal import on that very identification of Jesus as the Word who was God, and "without him was not any thing made that was made" (John 1:1–3). Ideas have no meaning without words, and words have no meaning without the ideas behind them. Language is one of the factors that concretely sets the human creature apart from the rest of creation. Note that God's first action recorded in Scripture is His speaking creation into existence.

All deviation from scriptural fact begins with a deviation from scriptural words. All error either adds to the words of God or subtracts from them. Any idea that attempts to change the words of God to suit the meaning of the moment or to gain acceptance by the ungodly, is in dangerous opposition to the omnipotent and omniscient God of creation.

Professional Jargon

Unique terms or jargon are used in every profession. The military uses adjective-laden phrases, while the government uses acronyms. Plumbers use specialized terms just as much as scientists. Technical descriptions (computer manuals, toy-assembly instructions) often assume a complete and comprehensive knowledge of a genre and expect the ordinary person to understand.

Obviously one cannot and should not eliminate all specialized terms. When speaking to a general audience, however, every professional should be able to communicate without using language that only the specialized can understand — that is, unless one wants to give the impression of superiority or has the intent to intimidate. In the theological world, the tendency is to use terms that only theologians know without clearly describing their meaning. Often, the effect forces the jargon-illiterate listener to give up trying to understand and to acquiesce to the intellectual prowess of the theologian. That very problem drove William Tyndale to translate the Bible from the original languages into the common English language so that every plowboy could read and understand God's eternal message — in spite of huge resistance from the religious community of the day.

In the netherworld of the conflict between evolutionary science and theology, those who disagree with what the Bible says will often resort to the "since-I-am-a-scientist . . ." argument. Books intended for the non-technical are loaded with technical terms, few of which are defined for the layman. This sends the message that since the technical concepts of the "scientist" are unquestionable, Bible words and biblical context must be understood in light of the "discoveries" of science. Therefore, in areas in which evolutionary science and biblical record conflict, one is essentially faced with believing the author of the book or the Author of *the* Book.

The apostle Paul insisted that his speech should demonstrate the Spirit's power rather than the enticing words of man's wisdom so that his hearers would base their faith in the power of God instead of in the wisdom of man.

> And I, brethren, when I came to you, came not with excellency of speech or of wisdom, declaring unto you the testimony of God. For I determined not to know any thing among you, save Jesus Christ, and him crucified. And I was with you in weakness, and in fear, and in much trembling. And my speech and my preaching was not with enticing words of man's wisdom, but in demonstration of the Spirit and of power: That your faith should not stand in the wisdom of men, but in the power of God (1 Cor. 2:1–5).

Obfuscation

Obfuscation is the technique of making the simple complex. Obfuscation makes the apparent bewildering. Obfuscation darkens the light and muddies up the clean and confuses the obvious. Obfuscation is a wonderful way to make an implausible case seem plausible.

Those who would graft long ages of death and struggle onto Scripture, use obfuscation in several ways. First and foremost, they insist that the simple words of Scripture cannot be understood merely by reading them. In many instances, a scientific expert claims that because we now know more than we ever did before, the Bible must be explained in light of what science has discovered. A lengthy discussion about why a particular Bible word does not mean what the word normally means will then follow. After that, the *expert* presents information which has come to light since the Bible was written and will (the expert would say) help us to understand what the Bible *really* means.

This shell game would be obvious to a Bible-believing Christian, but for the power of obfuscation!

By "making many books" (Eccles. 12:12), the obfuscator so intimidates the audience that his argument begins to sound correct. Solomon was one of the wisest men that ever lived. Check out what he said about the right way to use information:

> And moreover, because the preacher was wise, he still taught the people knowledge; yea, he gave good heed, and sought out, and set in order many proverbs. The preacher sought to find out acceptable words: and that which was written was upright, even words of truth. The words of the wise are as goads, and as nails fastened by the masters of assemblies, which are given from one shepherd (Eccles. 12:9–11).

Obfuscators do not follow Solomon's biblical formula.

The "Local Universal" Flood

A leading contender for the gold medal in hermeneutical gymnastics is the following passage from the works of a leading progressive creationist hybridizer:

> Behind this lengthy, though still incomplete, discussion of geological and other issues relating to the Flood

> lies a dual purpose: first, to offer a biblically consistent and scientifically plausible interpretation of the Flood account for any Bible reader; and, second, to remove one major barrier, the "geophysically impossible" global Flood, on which many skeptics rest their rejection of the Bible's message.
>
> Because this chapter covers so much material, a summary of the main points may prove helpful. These points all support the thesis that the Flood event described in Genesis 6–9 did, indeed, accomplish the ends God clearly intended — and explicitly stated — without covering the entire planet. It may be described, accurately, as universal (with respect to humans and the animals associated with them) but not as global.[5]

The first paragraphs certainly seem to assert noble goals: (1) offering a "biblically consistent and scientifically plausible interpretation of the Flood account," and (2) removing "one major barrier . . . on which many skeptics rest their rejection of the Bible's message."

Before acquiescing, consider these two points. First, imagine that all Christian leaders loudly and unitedly proclaimed, "We now realize the Bible does not teach a global Food; it is not necessary to believe in a global Flood to accept the Bible's message." Picture what would follow. With this "major barrier" removed, droves of scientifically literate 21st century Christians would exclaim, "At last I can believe the Bible's message. Since I don't have to believe the embarrassing, 'geophysically impossible' global Flood, now I can repent of my sins, accept being born again, rebuild my life on the new man created within me, look forward to God making a glorified body for me out of my rotting corpse, and rejoice at the coming dissolution of the universe by fire and the construction of a new heavens and a new earth that shall never know the death and struggle that helped create our present world!" Consider this also: if Christian leaders sell out the biblical record of the Flood to appease skeptics, on how many other biblical teachings must they sell out?

Secondly, take into account what must be done to the biblical text to usher in this massive conversion. In his first paragraph, the author claims to offer "a biblically consistent and scientifically plausible interpretation." Is his view biblically communicated or does he merely use biblical language in a manner only consistent with a view that begins and ends outside the Bible? Is the view he offers "scientifically acceptable" to the evolutionary establishment yet fundamentally at odds with the huge abundance of scientific evidence strongly supporting a geophysically necessary global Flood?

Re-read what is offered in the second paragraph: "the thesis that the Flood . . . did, indeed, accomplish the ends God clearly intended — and explicitly stated — without covering the entire planet. It may be described, accurately, as universal (with respect to humans and the animals associated with them) but not as global."

Incredibly, the author goes on to suggest that his universal flood covered only the Mesopotamian Valley, because God's penalty for Adam's sin (the curse on the ground) affected only mankind and his domestic animals, and these had multiplied (in over 1,500 years) only to fill the Tigris-Euphrates area.

Now, re-read Genesis 3:17–19 (God's curse on the ground for Adam's sin) and Genesis 6–9 on the Flood. Note how the powerful words of Scripture are diametrically opposed to the interpretation softened to satisfy secular skeptics:

a. God's punishment for Adam's sin extended far beyond Adam's spirit and body (spiritual and physical death). It is a curse on the ground, the element substance of the universe, that caused the ground to bring forth thorns and thistles and the heavens to grow old and wear out like a garment! Likewise the final consummation of all things in Christ provides new heavens and a new earth, not just restoration of mankind and his domestic animals!

b. God's displeasure with the world after Eden extended far beyond farms and farmers in the Fertile Crescent (Gen. 6:7, 13): "And the Lord said, I will destroy man whom I have created from the face of the earth; both man, and beast, and the creeping thing, and the fowls of the air; for it repenteth me that I have made them. And God said unto Noah, The end of all flesh is come before me; for the earth is filled with violence through them; and, behold, I will destroy them with the earth."

c. God uses unusually extravagant and repetitive language to describe the destruction of dry land animal life in the Flood. He repeats phrases referring to all flesh four times: "And all flesh died that moved upon the earth" (Gen. 7:21). "All in whose nostrils was the breath of life, of all that was in the dry land, died" (Gen. 7:22). "And every living substance was destroyed which was upon the face of the ground" (Gen. 7:23). To make sure no one could possibly miss the point, God describes the life that died by listing the particular animal groups twice: "both of fowl, and of cattle, and of beast, and of every creeping thing that creepeth upon the earth [the domesticated lizards and snakes?], and every man" (Gen. 7:21); "both man, and cattle, and the creeping things, and the fowl of the heaven" (Gen. 7:23). God then summarizes the biological extent of the Flood in two phrases, one negative and one positive, the first describing what died: "they [the every living substance and the list of animals just given] were destroyed from the earth [not from just the Tigris-Euphrates Valley, words which were available to God, and would have been understood]" (Gen. 7:23). Summarizing the extent of the Flood positively, God then positively describes what life survived: "and Noah only remained alive, and they that were with him in the ark" (Gen. 7:23).

d. Genesis also describes the geologic/geographic extent of the Flood in extravagant and repetitive — and global — language, Genesis 7:17–20 builds a dramatic picture: "the waters increased and bare up the ark"; "the waters prevailed, and were increased greatly upon the earth"; "the waters prevailed exceedingly upon the earth" [not, "and reached toward the rim of the valley"!]. Verses 19–20 continue dramatically, with two double emphases: "and all the high hills [not just hills], that were under the whole heaven [not just heaven, or heavens visible to Noah!], were covered" over to a depth of 15 cubits (about 22 ft. or nearly 7 m). This shows that the ark could have floated over the highest mountain without touching bottom: "Fifteen cubits upward did the waters prevail; and the mountains were covered."

e. Why would God have Noah build a huge ark to escape the rising waters of a valley flood? Would God also have to build a fence around the valley to keep people (and their domestic animals) from just walking away during the several months it took the Flood to crest? Christ compares the judgment by fire to come with the judgment at Noah's time (2 Pet. 3). Does that mean God will then set fire to a huge valley, the new heavens will be what we see when the smoke clears, and the new earth, the lush regrowth of vegetation in the ash fertilized soil? Of course, progressive creationists do not believe that — but why not? Whether by ignorance of science and Scripture, overzealousness for the praises of men, or sincerely well-intentioned desire to make it easier for skeptics to accept Christ, the "universal local flood" concept so belittles the nature and extent of God's judgment and Christ's restoration that it borders on blasphemy.

This list is just a summary of obvious biblical issues. Other books and articles deal with the "micro-errors" of progressive creationism — misusing the Hebrew language, defending all evolutionary antagonism to a global Flood against the real scientific evidence that supports a global Flood, and presenting "straw man" arguments against post-Flood biological diversification that really fits nicely with the Bible narrative literally — just as God wrote it!

The "mega-errors" of progressive creationism, some cited above, are obvious to someone who compares the words and concepts of a progressive creationist with the words and concepts of Scripture. That is how the Berean Christians "checked out" the apostle Paul. They did not argue with his knowledge of Hebrew language or history or of Greek language or philosophy. They checked the foundation upon which he was building, to determine whether or not his preaching was rooted and grounded in the basic words and principles of the Word of God.

If the root is rotten, do not eat the fruit!

Good Fruit from a Rotten Root?

A basic principle cited many times in Scripture is that a bitter spring cannot produce sweet water (James 3:11). Blessing and cursing should not come from the same mouth (James 3:10). Grapes cannot be gathered from figs, nor good figs from a bad root (James 3:12).

When Christian leaders are in disagreement, many Christians seem to throw up their hands and say "How can I ever sort through all these complex arguments?" There is a biblical short-cut, the Berean short-cut: Look for the foundation. On what foundation are the complex arguments erected? What basic reason is given (or assumed) for suggesting an interpretation different from a straightforward reading of God's Word?

The list of quotes below consists of several well-known and highly respected Christian leaders. These quotations are not meant to impugn the Christian character of those quoted, nor their contributions in other areas of biblical understanding. The quotations are presented simply to show that hybrid theologies regarding origins are based solidly and unswervingly on commitment to long ages of death and struggle as the "fact" which must determine how we understand Genesis. If the hybrid foundation is wrong, it does not really matter how cleverly built or beautifully adorned the structure is. It does not matter how many people praise and admire the construction. Cathedrals built on the shifting sands of man's opinion do not honor God.

Genesis is the foundation for the Bible's creation-Fall-redemption theme. If the foundation is rotten, do NOT climb the stairs to admire the view.

- It is apparent that the most straightforward understanding of the Genesis record, without regard to all of the hermeneutical considerations suggested by science, is that God created heaven and earth in six solar days, that man was created in the sixth day, that death and chaos entered the world after the Fall of Adam and Eve. (Pattle Pun)[6]

- From a superficial reading of Genesis 1, the impression received is that the entire creative process took place in six 24-hour days. If this was the true intent of the Hebrew author (a questionable deduction, as will be presently shown), this seems to run counter to modern scientific research, which indicates that the planet Earth was created several billion years ago. (Gleason Archer)[7]

- It is of course admitted that, taking this account by itself, it would be most natural to understand the word [day] in its ordinary sense; but if that sense brings the Mosaic account into conflict with facts, and another sense avoids such conflict, then it is obligatory on us to adopt that other. (Charles Hodge)[8]

- Hitchcock concluded that even though newer interpretations of the biblical narrative did not seem to be "the most natural meaning," yet if geological facts "unequivocally require such an interpretation to harmonize the Bible with nature," then "science must be allowed to modify our exegesis of Scripture." (Davis Young quoting Edward Hitchcock)[9]

- In this article, I have advocated an interpretation of biblical cosmogony according to which Scripture is open to the current scientific view of a very old universe and, in that respect, does not discountenance the theory of the evolutionary origin of man. (Meredith Kline)[10]

In contrast, consider Martin Luther's words:

> When Moses writes that God created heaven and earth and whatever is in them in six days, then let this period continue to have been six days, and do not venture to devise any comment according to which six days were one day. But if you cannot understand how this could have been done in six days, then grant the Holy Spirit the honor of being more learned than you are. For you are to deal with Scripture in such a way that you bear in mind that God himself says what is written. But since God is speaking, it is not fitting for you wantonly to turn His Word in the direction you wish to go.[11]

Itching Ears

The Bible contains abundant warnings to those who would follow false teaching. All of the warnings are sober, and all reveal the awful consequences for those who fail to test man's word by comparing it with the inerrant words of God. One such warning appears in 2 Timothy:

> For the time will come when they will not endure sound doctrine; but after their own lusts shall they heap to themselves teachers, having itching ears; And they shall turn away their ears from the truth, and shall be turned unto fables (2 Tim. 4:3–4).

Unfortunately, many professing Christians have a weakness for the world and a desire for its pleasures, including even a longing for "intellectual respectability" and the praises of men. The words of Scripture about "dying to self" are clear enough, but too unpleasant. Their ears "itch" to hear a different message, a message that promotes their own peace, prosperity, and praise — a message (like the one that beguiled Eve) that would make them like God, determining for themselves what God's words really mean.

More unfortunately, there are false teachers more than willing to scratch that itch — would-be teachers with itching ears themselves, itching to hear what the people want and anxious to give it to them, even if it means justifying sinful cravings.

Although momentarily soothed by false doctrine, the itch returns, demanding more false doctrine, which is eagerly supplied — a self-feeding spiral suffocating Scripture and sucking adherents into the cesspool of Satan's lies and Satan's fate.

Those with itching ears are "corrupted from the simplicity that is in Christ" (2 Cor. 11:3). The only salve which cures the itch forever is the sincere milk of the Word (1 Pet. 2:2).

> Fear not them which kill the body, but are not able to kill the soul: but rather fear him which is able to destroy both soul and body in hell (Matt. 10:28).

Endnotes

1 Robert Kolker, "High Caliber Justice," includes an interview with Jack B. Weinstein, in *New York Magazine*, April 5, 1999, www.newyorkmetro.com (accessed October 7, 2003).

2 Office of the Independent Council, Referral to the United States House of Representatives pursuant to Title 28, United States Code, 595 (c) by Kenneth W. Starr, September 9, 1998, http://icrreports.access.gpo.gov/report/6narrit.htm#L8 (accessed October 15, 2003).

3 Elizabeth Shogren and Richard A. Serrano, "Nation Views Clinton's Taped Testimony Before Grand Jury," *Los Angeles Times*, September 22, 1998, Online: < http://www.latimes.com/HOME/NEWS/REPORTS/SCANDAL/STORIES/lat_main0922.htm> (accessed September 10, 2003).

4 Allan Menzies, ed., introduction to "Origen," in *Recently Discovered Additions to Early Christian Literature; Commentaries of Origen,* Vol.

10, "Early Church Fathers," http://www.cel.org/fathers2/ANF-10/anf10-34.htm#P6048-898080 (accessed October 15, 2003).

5 Hugh Ross, *The Genesis Question* (Colorado Springs, CO: Navpress, 1998), p. 155.

6 Pattle P.T. Pun, "A Theology of Progressive Creationism," *Perspectives on Science and Christian Faith* 39 (March 1987): 9-19.

7 Gleason L. Archer Jr., *A Survey of Old Testament Introduction* (Chicago, IL: Moody Press, 1974), p. 181–182.

8 Charles Hodge, *Systematic Theology*, Vol. 1 (Grand Rapids, MI: Wm. B. Eerdmans Publishing Co., 1952), p. 570–571.

9 Davis A. Young, *The Biblical Flood* (Grand Rapids, MI: Wm B Eerdmans Publishing Co., 1995), p. 146, quoting Edward Hitchcock.

10 Meredith G. Kline, "Space and Time in the Genesis Cosmogony," *Perspectives on Science and Christian Faith* 48 (March 1996): 15 n. 47.

11 Ewald M. Plass, compiler, *What Luther Says: An Anthology*, Vol. 3 (St. Louis, MO: Concordia Publishing House, 1959), p. 1523, quoting Martin Luther.

Chapter 13

Lean Not to Your Own Understanding

The evolutionary philosophy of "up from the beasts" certainly seems irreconcilable with the Christian view of "fall from Paradise," and our whole view of history will certainly be determined by which way we believe![1]

— Hieromonk Seraphim Rose (1934–1982)

This look at the world after Eden began with the sad story of Charles Templeton, a once-renowned evangelist whose faith in the biblical God of creation was progressively eroded until finally he wrote:

> I believe that there is no supreme being with human attributes — no God in the biblical sense — but that all life is the result of timeless evolutionary forces, having reached its present transient state over millions of years.[2]

Mountains of evidence made evolution a fact to Templeton — a fact that made God fiction. "Science falsely so called" caused Templeton to turn from the good news of new life in Christ.

May God be praised that many other stories run in the opposite direction, from belief in millions of years of death and struggle to saving faith and new life in Jesus Christ. For some, however, such a transition has taken them from insisting that time, chance, struggle, and death brought man and other animals into existence to agreeing that one could believe the Bible and evolution at the same time.

Stopping at that position, however, yields more confusion. The Bible and evolution together? What kind of God would call millions of years of struggle and death very good? What kind of God would make billions of mistakes and bury His mistakes as fossils under the thousands of feet of rock worldwide? Who would pray to a God who wiped out 99 percent of all the species He supposedly created?

Thankfully, some conversion stories do not stop with a belief in both the Bible and evolution. God's Word clears up the confusion by pointing out that struggle, death, and the war of nature were man's fault, not God's, the result of the curse on the ground for mankind's sin and rebellion. The violence and corruption that filled the earth after man's sin in Eden brought on God's judgment as the worldwide flood in Noah's time. Jesus is not a God who worked through millions of years of struggle and death. One who could raise the dead by the words of His power was a God of miracles, a God who did not need millions of years of trial and error or experimentation to accomplish His purposes; and He was not a God who would renege on His promise to restore the universe to its Edenic perfection.

What Does God's Nature Teach Us?

Even though God proclaimed His creation good during the creation week, the universe gives evidence of much evil. How can we separate the original good from the fallen evil? The overwhelming majority of the Bible deals with the redemption of the creation — an age-long plan of God to bring about a new heavens and a new earth that is in total submission to His holiness (2 Pet. 3:13). How do we sort out the differences? What does the revealed nature of God furnish that will permit us to evaluate the distinction between evolutionary theories and God's description of creation? Perhaps a quick review of the attributes of God will help:

- *God is holy; He cannot lie.*
  However we describe the methodology of creation, we cannot imply that God is deceitful about His work in nature. For instance, it would not fit the nature of

God to suggest that He deceived us about the order of the creation week. It would not fit to have God telling us one thing, and then to have us find out something opposite through our science. Whatever we conclude, it must agree with the holiness of God.

- *God is omniscient: He is not unaware of anything.*
  He does not guess, nor does He use trial-and-error methodology. It would not fit God's character, for instance, for Him to need for nature to run amok — without any direction or purpose — in order for the right sequence of events to finally occur. God does not need nature to experiment for Him. However we explain the processes of the universe, those explanations must acquiesce to the omniscience of God.

- *God is love.*
  It would not fit God to exploit the senseless death of trillions of life forms just to accomplish what He wanted to achieve all along. God could not use the wasteful and cruel processes of naturalistic evolution to create a universe that would speak the invisible nature of His godhead. When we try to unravel the story of what God did in ages past, we must tell the story with God's love as a main ingredient.

- *God's universe displays order and purpose. God has a specific plan.*
  It would be contradictory to the nature of God for Him to create the myriads of misfits and sometimes grotesque creatures we see in the fossil record. If His purpose was to bring glory to himself and to have eternal fellowship with man, however we define the universe around us, we must define it in terms of the design and order of God.

- *God is an omnipresent Spirit.*
  He is not nature. He is not the universe. He is not a cosmic consciousness or a force of mystery. He cannot

be compared to the mystic "it" of Eastern religions. Personification of forces is not consistent with the God of Scripture.

More could be said! Many books, entire theological courses, and hours of personal study are devoted to plumbing the inexhaustible depth of God's attributes. Finite man will never fully comprehend the nature of God, but we must superimpose His revealed character on any attempt to speak of His creation. We may never fully understand how God formed the creation — man can never speak anything into existence — but we must apply the Creator's character to descriptions of the world that now exists. Using the guidelines of God's attributes, we can develop a reliable filter that will help us to evaluate human efforts to explain the present.

Understanding God's Nature Brings Clarity

It is understanding who God was, who Adam was, what the real nature and extent of sin is, and why severance of the relationship between the Creator and creation's chief steward had cosmic consequences that brings clarity. Even though man turned away from God, God did not turn away from man, but rather sent His own Son, Jesus Christ, to pay the penalty for man's sin and to conquer death.

Charles Templeton came to believe that accepting the Bible as God's Word was "intellectual suicide" that kept him from a "life of unrestricted thought." Others believe that accepting the Bible as God's Word sets them free from the vagaries of human opinion, lifting them far above the limits of time, space, and culture and giving them a rock-solid foundation and eternal perspective! Templeton believed God's Word made a prison wall; others believe God's Word sets them free. They use God's Word to evaluate human opinion, and find it difficult to imagine why any Christian would trust the words of "experts" to interpret the words of God. God's never-changing Word saves them from man's ever-changing words!

Evolutionists and atheists (and compromisers) are horrified and mystified by the growing acceptance of biblical creationism among those with strong backgrounds in science. That really should not be surprising, since scientists study God's world, and what they see in God's world agrees with what they read in God's Word. What they see makes it hard to believe in evolution — or in long ages of death, struggle, and "progressive creation."

The exquisite design, persistence of the criteria for classification, and initial complexity and diversity of each group make the fossilized organisms look like descendants of kinds produced by plan, purpose, and special acts of creation. The evidence of disease and predation among the fossils, plus their obvious death, point back to the "bondage of corruption" that followed Adam's sin. Even evolutionists teach that the overwhelming majority of fossils were formed by rapid, deep burial — flood conditions. The continent-wide width and great depth of fossil deposits in ecosedimentary zones with gaps of millions of mythical years missing between them suggest nothing short of a continent-wide, mountain-covering worldwide flood catastrophe as described in Genesis. The recent, rapid, re-filling of the earth with diversified descendants of the people and animals aboard the ark even provides a picture of the final deliverance from judgment ushered in by the blessed return of Christ.

Could it really be a six-day creation a few thousand years ago?

Academics can tolerate ideas of creation (so long as they are not too biblical) and can even accept the evidence for worldwide catastrophe (so long as there are several worldwide disasters with millions of years between them), but belief in a six-day creation a few thousand years old can mean the end of academic respectability (even in many Christian circles). Unfortunately, due to this, many people feel impressed with their understanding while being buried in the quagmire of expert opinion. To commit to God's words, or not to commit, that is the question. The most dramatic part of many conversions is the rejection — consciously and deliberately — of personal opinions in favor of God's clear and simple words (Prov. 3:4–6; Isa. 55:8–9). God said six days, went out of His way to emphasize six days, and even gave us reasons from other Scriptures and from science to accept six days as — literally — six days. Building the understanding of God's world on God's Word and tapping into the infinite wisdom of God, why then should the believer slide back into the quagmire and try to build an understanding of the universe on the infinitesimal wisdom of man.

Interpretation Can Be a Slippery Slope

Remember Dan Barker's story in chapter 1? A minister and writer of two popular Christian musicals who once proudly waved the Bible as humanity's standard, Dan recorded his slide down the slippery slope of interpretation in his book, *Losing Faith in Faith*:

> I used to believe that Adam and Eve were literal. . . . But I got to thinking that there are parts of the Bible that are obviously metaphorical. . . . My first tiny step away from fundamentalism [i.e., biblical literalism] was . . . to realize that it shouldn't matter to me whether other Christians held it historically. . . . Sounds silly, but that was a big step in the direction of tolerance [accepting man's opinion on the same level of authority as God's Word]. . . .
>
> After a couple of years I migrated further. . . .
>
> To my list of religious metaphors, which included the Prodigal Son and Adam and Eve, I now added God.[3]

The "first tiny step" developed into a giant leap as Dan Barker "migrated further," finally making God a "metaphor" and surrendering his public faith for public atheism. He is now the public relations director for the Freedom ***From*** Religion Foundation [emphasis added].

The problem with interpretation, from Eve in the Garden onward, has always been to know when to quit giving man's words authority over God's Word.

Which doctrine will we interpret, which words will we plasticize, to make Christianity palatable to the (supposedly) scientifically literate 21st-century Christian? Perhaps a six-day creation seems more ridiculous than a virgin birth, but what about Lazarus' rotting corpse coming to life . . . or the lame walking, blind seeing, or lepers instantly being cured? Is the whole idea of bodily resurrection as ludicrous to 21st-century scientists as it was to the Sadducees in Jesus' time?

Why should we interpret Scripture to accommodate only the natural sciences? Consider Paul's warning about false teachers and itching ears (2 Tim. 4:3–4). False teachers tell the crowd what they want to hear (in soothing biblical language, of course), and the crowd praises those who so teach — which enables them to speak to larger crowds, which. . . . Both are on the broad way, entering through the wide gate. "There is a way which seemeth right unto a man, but the end thereof are the ways of death" (Prov. 14:12).

Remember from the preface Eugenie Scott's concession to Hugh Ross's approach to science? Ross is a leading spokesman for the progressive creation movement, and Scott is leading an all-out effort to remove every vestige of Christianity from the American consciousness. Obviously, she does not endorse Ross's God, nor is she trying to lure him from his faith. She is willing instead, it seems, to wait for the next generation. For the anti-Christian lawyers united with others for "separation of church and state" (read that "separation of Christianity from society"), the battle is for our children and the future. Scott seems to be betting (and, ironically it is a wager with a solid biblical basis) that a little compromise in this generation will lead to more in the next. If Christian compromisers and atheistic evolutionists both agree that long ages of death and struggle are true, then the next generation will see that they are true regardless of what "God says" or even whether or not God exists. Eugenie Scott and her ilk seem to realize that Christian leaders with a martyr's faith in long ages of death and struggle are greasing the slippery slope that leads from worship of the Creator to worship of the creature, and from faith to ____________ ("foolishness" is the biblical term; "enlightenment" is Lucifer's term).

How can we reverse the slippery slide down the slippery slope? The power must come from God — but how? Remember the conversation between Billy Graham and Charles Templeton in chapter 1. Having rejected biblical creation in favor of evolution's long ages of death and struggle, Templeton finally slid all the way to the bottom, making evolution itself the creator in the place of Christ. Billy refused to step onto that slippery slope, saying:

> I believe the Genesis account of creation because it's in the Bible.

There is the ANSWER: take the Bible literally . . . proclaim it as the Word of God!

Power to the Pastor! Power to the Pew!

Such logic is certainly not subtle or sophisticated, just simple. Take God at His Word, and let God's power do the rest.

That is the kind of simplicity God wants us to have: taking God at His Word and using our intelligence — and His Spirit — to put His words into practice. The Bible puts it this way: [God] makes wise the simple (Ps. 19:7) and brings the wisdom of the proud to naught (Ps. 33:10).

The power comes from looking at the world through God's eyes, not from looking at God through the world's eyes.

The Bible's words and foundational concepts are so clear and so clearly communicated that the simple who are wise in Christ can examine the experts to see if they are building on the right foundation, the only sure foundation. *As Eve found out the very hard way, no matter how tempting the fruit, do not eat it if the tree's roots are rotten!*

As much as ever before, Christian leaders and laymen need the Berean attitude (Acts 17). For leaders, that means building on the sure foundation of God's Word and communicating clearly, zealous to be understood and to bring glory to God's words not their own. For laymen, that means the burning desire to search the Scriptures to see if these things be so, both checking the "root stock" of the experts and also bringing God's Word to bear on social issues, even if it means standing up to ridicule.

Take God at His Word, and act on it! "For my thoughts are not your thoughts, neither are your ways my ways, saith the Lord. For as the heavens are higher than the earth, so are my ways higher than your ways, and my thoughts than your thoughts" (Isa. 55:8–9). When testing the wisdom of men's words against the wisdom of God's Word, keep the following points in mind.

Genesis chapters 1–11 are vitally important.

The father of lies has been particularly effective in convincing the church that the origin and history of the universe and life on earth is an academic side issue, a source of confusion in the church that is best left to experts in science.

- Genesis 1–11 is the intensely practical record of beginnings. It describes not only the origin of the universe, earth, life, and man, but also the origin — and, hence, the meaning, purpose, and value — of the communion between God and man (Creator and creature), of mankind's role as chief steward of God's creature, of the husband-wife relationship, of the interaction and interdependence of different parts of the creation. It records also the corruption of creation through the origin of sin, death, struggle, thorns and thistles, pain, Darwin's "war of nature," and the age-long war between Satan and the seed of the woman. It records the catastrophic worldwide judgment of Noah's flood, and the origin afterward of tribes, tongues, nations (not "races"), government, and culture. Most blessedly, it also records God's promise to redeem all creation, and the early unfolding of that most magnificent plan (Logos).
- Without Genesis 1-11, we would be left to the vagaries of human opinion to explain the origin, meaning, purpose and value of worship, stewardship, marriage, family, sin, death, government, languages, nations, and the need for Christ's coming, perfect life, death, resurrection, and coming again!

The historicity of Genesis 1-11 provides a solid basis for worldwide Christian evangelism.

There is one "race," the human race, which are all descended from one pair of parents created by the one triune God. All peoples have the same origin, the same problem — sin — and the same solution — salvation in Jesus Christ, the Son of the one who created all peoples! Since Genesis 1–11 is real history, there is no need nor place for the myth and misfortune of cultural relativism and the politically correct "toleration" (i.e., acceptance as equally valid) for the many paths to gods of our own making.

Genesis 1–11 enables us to understand both evil and evolution.

There are things wrong with the world that need to be set right. Genesis 1–11 explains the origin of evil in man's heart and the origin of time, chance, struggle, and death in man's domain. It was Adam's sin, not God's creative acts, that brought spiritual and physical death and a curse on the ground. The evolutionary process, Darwin's "war of nature," is all too real in the present world, but it makes things worse, not better — explaining the origin of disease, disease organisms, and defects, but not the origin of "new and improved" types. Because of man's sin, there is struggle and death now, but — praise God — there were no long ages of death and struggle before the first Adam's sin, nor will they be present after the Last Adam's return.

What we read in God's Word agrees with what we see in God's world.

Psalm 19:1–4 says all peoples are surrounded by a convincing but "silent sermon" in which "the heavens declare the glory of God, and the firmament shows forth His handywork." Romans 1:18–20 says that the godhead's eternal power and deity is so clearly seen in all the things that have been made that people are without excuse. This "natural revelation" does not point vaguely to some "creative force" in nature itself; it points to the transcendent, eternally existent God of the Bible as Creator, sustainer, Judge, and Redeemer.

- Features of interdependence and "irreducible complexity" point to the special, completed supernatural acts in the past by which God as Creator established patterns of order in the universe and the first of each kind of life, including mankind. Regular, continuing, "natural" processes in the present, discoverable by the methods of science, represent the "laws" that describe how God is the daily, faithful sustainer of all this creation (Col. 1:17). Suffering and death, "nature, red in tooth and claw," billions of dead things buried as fossils in rock layers all over the earth, exploding stars, and the heavens growing old and wearing out like a garment — all these things testify that God is Judge, the one who cursed the ground as the penalty for Adam's sin. But, praise God, in the healing work of Christ, we see God's power as Redeemer, the one who forgives sin, restores life, and who will set the whole creation free of its "bondage of corruption," so that the creation itself will obtain "the glorious liberty of the children of God" (Rom. 8:21).
- Both nature and nature's God tell of God's perfect creation, ruined by man's sin, destroyed by the Flood, and which will be restored to new life in Jesus.

God's Word interprets God's world — not the other way around.

It is the height of folly and arrogance to believe that the ever-changing words of men hold the key to understanding the never-changing Word of God — especially since man's brain has suffered 6,000 years of the curse, his heart is "deceitful above all things, and desperately wicked" (Jer. 17:9), and "every imagination of the thoughts of his heart [is] only evil continually" (Gen. 6:5).

- Imagine watching a television drama on mute. It is extremely difficult to figure out the plot and sometimes hard to tell the "good guys" from the "bad guys." Now imagine listening to a drama on the car radio. The plot and purpose are clear, and the imagination fills in the pictures easily. "Facts" do not speak for themselves; words do!

- Observations, even objectively repeatable and verifiable scientific observations do NOT speak for themselves; they need a "spokesperson" (scientist) to interpret their meaning or significance — and the interpretation is no better, broader, or more reliable than the motives, experiences, and skill of their interpreter. God's words interpret God's world in terms of the omniscience, omnipotence, and infinite wisdom and care of its transcendent Creator! What believer would ever consider using man's words to interpret God's Word, which is forever settled in heaven (Ps. 119:89)?

Experimental/empirical science is an excellent tool for exploring the present world.

By restricting itself to formulating and testing ideas on the basis of repeatable and objectively verifiable observations of present data and processes, experimental science has discovered patterns of order and made and used predictive statements (theories) about nature that properly earn our respect.

But empirical science, deriving its strength from restricting itself to repeatable observations in the present, cannot describe conditions in either the unobserved past or the unforeseeable future. Biblical revelation lifts us above the limits of space and time in the present, and gives us God's account of ultimate origins past and ultimate destiny future!

- As concepts of ultimate origins, both evolution and creation models lie far beyond the purview of science. However, testable deductions can be made on the basis of either models — and scientific tests have repeatedly falsified evolutionary deductions and supported those based on biblical perspective.

- Originally based on the biblical world view, science is not, not, NOT the enemy of the Christian faith; science is the Christian's ally in its battle with evolution.

Evolution is not science; it is humanism dressed up in a lab coat.

Evolution is not science, never was science, never will be science, and never could be science. Evolution is a belief about the past made up by men who were not there — men who are limited and finite, men who do not have all the evidence, men who have made a great many mistakes in the past about the past. Dressed up in scientific jargon to pirate true science's respectability, evolution is merely a deification of human opinion, an example of the "science falsely so called" about which the Bible warns us because by professing it, some have "erred concerning the faith" (1 Tim. 6:20–21).

Long ages of death and struggle are the non-negotiable core of the evolutionist's faith.

The evolutionary process is pictured as chance changes in heredity (mutations) culled by struggle and death (Darwin's "war of nature" or "natural selection"). Chance, struggle, and death do play roles in a creation corrupted by sin, but evolutionists believe these processes ultimately produce better adapted and more varied life forms. Even evolutionists believe that it would take enormous amounts of time for chance, struggle, and death to produce progressive development — and that presumes evolutionists will someday overcome the solid scientific evidence against their unwarranted extrapolation.

Christian compromisers today try to force long ages of death and struggle into the Bible.

Even compromising Christians often agree that the words of Scripture describe a six-day creation, no death before Adam's sin, a worldwide Flood, and a new heavens and earth at Christ's return. Nevertheless, they universally assert that the so-called fact of long ages of death and struggle require a new interpretation, one that hybridizes the biblical message with what they call science.

- Theistic evolutionists often say that evolution is true "scientifically" and the Bible is true "spiritually." They may assume God used evolution to create, but regardless, they see science and faith as different spheres of knowledge that cannot be in conflict. Since the Bible clearly, continually, and consistently bases the life and work of Jesus in historical reality, it is surprising that a Christian would be interested in this view — yet many are, in spite of the fact that the view works just as well for Hindus, Buddhists, Muslims, or agnostics. "Crediting" the Father of Jesus with using millions of years of death and struggle to create things makes it difficult to believe He would send His Son to conquer the death and struggle He considered very good for millions of years.
- Gap theorists at least blame death and struggle on Satan, not God, by putting Lucifer's fall and millions of horrible years into a supposed gap between Genesis 1:1 and 1:2. Neither science nor Scripture support that view, and it still puts struggle, death, and disaster into the world God called very good. Gap theorists may, however, believe in a six-day "re-creation" and a global Flood.
- Progressive creationism and other "day-age" theories are having the biggest impact — and doing the most harm — because they claim man's "science" demands a new interpretation of the "creation days," then they use one or the other of such interpretations to stand publicly against the literal reading of Genesis 1–11.

Nature is definitely not "the 67th book of the Bible"

Satan usually adds, subtracts, or twists only a few of God's words at a time in violation of the scriptural command not to add to or take away from God's Word. Taken literally, adding a whole book, as suggested by progressive creationist Hugh Ross, would be the height of heresy! No doubt, Ross only means that God reveals himself in His world as well as His Word — but then he gets the "spectacles of Scripture" on backwards.

Ross tries to interpret the words of God using man's words about God's world. God's words speak for themselves, and they speak God's truth. Nature cannot speak for itself, but only "says" what the corrupted mind and heart of sinful man makes it say! God is His own interpreter, and it is the self-interpreting words (i.e., literal reading) of the 66 books of the Bible that enable us to correctly understand God's revelation in His world!

- Letting human opinion usurp the authority of God's Word repeats Eve's sin, and denies both the power and love of God.
- Claiming that only "experts" can correctly understand God's Word creates a "priesthood" of the scientific elite that undoes the Reformation and rending of the temple veil, and ignores the fact that all are equally ignorant before God!
- While claiming to interpret Scripture in the light of "science," progressive creationists and day-age hybridizers often ignore genuine scientific research that supports Scripture and simply "baptize" beliefs about science acceptable to evolutionists.
- Applied to other Scriptures, the "hermeneutical gymnastics" required to make the six days of creation into something else could be used to twist, contort, or deny each and every teaching of Scriptures — even making the life, death, and "resurrection" of Christ a myth, allegory, or "spiritual story." It is very hard to tell the difference between compromise hermeneutics and the outright rejection of God's words by those who do not know the God who is speaking. They have no desire to find out more about Him because they are spiritually blind.

- The "Galileo episode" was not a fight between science and the Bible. Instead, a compromising church was defending pagan philosophy against a truth from God's world which was consistent with God's Word. History should not repeat itself!

It is the Word, not the world, that brings conviction and conversion.

Some day-age compromises may be only pandering to the praises of men (like false teachers with itching ears), but others sincerely believe that accommodating Scripture to long ages of death and struggle will (a) make the salvation message more palatable to the scientifically literate, and/or (b) make loss of faith less likely for naive Christians when they are finally exposed to the "facts of science" (i.e., the evolutionary interpretation of science).

Certainly one can sympathize with the desire to induce or preserve faith. But the faith that saves from the world, and the faith that lasts, is the faith anchored in the sure foundation of God's Word!

When Paul preached Christ's resurrection to the sophisticated Greek intellectuals on Mars Hill, they laughed. He came back, NOT with an academically palatable interpretation of the Resurrection, but with a return to the basics the Greeks had forgotten — the facts that God created mankind and that man rebelled against God. Against this background of God's creation and man's sin, Christ's redemptive work made sense. Some still laughed; some wanted to hear more; and some believed (Acts 17).

What Did Salvation Accomplish?

What did Jesus accomplish on the Cross? Did He secure salvation for mankind only, or was His death also a part of the payment that would ultimately free creation from the death cycle? What about man's body? Did the sacrifice of Christ's body secure man's resurrection, or was it merely a symbol of the "greater spiritual truth" of an allegorical act? These questions examine the heart of Christianity.

The salvation (new birth) given to us by God provides four foundational platforms upon which believers build — platforms upon which they structure the new life. Without clearly understanding these basic attributes, we will not be able to properly use or adequately apply what God has granted.

God's salvation is unconditional and free.

God's gifts are absolutely free — to us. Like everything else that God does for us, birth into His family is not earnable. We do not deserve His gift, nor can we ever do something to be worthy of His gift. He gives us His gift because He loves us. This gift of eternal life (the same kind of life that the resurrected Christ has) is given freely to anyone who will believe in what God has said and done to restore the perfect relationship once held by the created and the Creator. This grace, first experienced personally in the granting of salvation, is the basis for all of the power that God gives to us to use now and in our eternal life.

Once granted, God's gift is complete and eternal.

If words mean anything, "eternal" life must not be "temporary." If nothing but God's grace is the basis for the granting of the gift, then how can any human work play a part? If we must simply believe to receive God's gift, then how could obedience or any other factor be required? Man does not earn it. Man does not "turn it on or off." Man merely *receives* it, under the conditions defined by the giver.

The belief requires a belief in God's Word and in God's ability to do what He says. The focus of the belief is directed toward the sacrifice of Jesus Christ as the willing substitute for our sins. He took our sin *and* our place. He endured the judgment and punishment that we deserved. He satisfied God's perfect requirement and gave His infinite, sinless life in the stead of our eternal condemnation, and did all that was necessary to rescue us from damnation if we believe.

It would therefore follow, and does follow in Scripture, that if man has nothing to do with saving himself, then he has nothing to do with keeping himself saved.

> Blessed be the God and Father of our Lord Jesus Christ, which according to his abundant mercy hath begotten us again unto a lively hope by the resurrection of Jesus Christ from the dead, To an inheritance incorruptible, and undefiled, and that fadeth not away, reserved in heaven for you, Who are kept by the power of God through faith unto salvation ready to be revealed in the last time (1 Pet. 1:3–5).

Once again, if one believes in an omnipotent, omniscient, Creator who brought everything into existence in perfect harmony with His perfection, it is not difficult to trust this all-powerful Creator to create a new being "in righteousness and true holiness" (Eph. 4:24).

Adopting the viewpoint of the progressive creationist, however, brings uncertainty and doubt about the character of God's nature and His Word. If we are continually plagued with the accuracy of God's message to us, we will find it difficult to appropriate the wonderful authority that God has made available to us as we live the Christian life. With constant doubt in our hearts about the love of God toward us, we can hardly pray with confidence, resist the Evil One, or maintain a victorious life of joy. As the writer to the Hebrews insisted, the foundational confidence of our faith lies in our belief regarding the creation account.

- **Once implemented, God's salvation supplies the spiritual power that we do not have.**

It would seem utterly foolish for God to design a salvation that could only be achieved by His omnipotent intervention, and then leave the ones to whom He granted this indescribable gift to fend alone in a world that is dominated by evil. He would not expect us to understand and obey His will if His message to us was so unclear that we would have to depend on secular science for us to comprehend it. Since the Fall and ensuing Curse, mankind has existed in a "dead" condition, functioning in a universe that groans and travails in pain. We are saddled with our fallen nature — and will be until the universe itself is redeemed. Fortunately, the salvation secured by Jesus Christ makes possible a complete victory over that "dead" condition.

> According as his divine power hath given unto us all things that pertain unto life and godliness, through the knowledge of him that hath called us to glory and virtue. Whereby are given unto us exceeding great and precious promises: that by these ye might be partakers of the divine nature, having escaped the corruption that is in the world through lust (2 Pet. 1:3–4).

Note the certain and specific promises in those verses. We are given everything we need for life and godliness; we are given great and precious promises; we are able to participate in the divine nature; and we are able to escape the corruption in the world — ultimately including the physical corruption of our bodies in death. If words mean anything, God has made it possible for us to live a victorious life in this world. He has given us everything that we need to share in His nature and to escape the corruption that naturally draws us away from Him.

When salvation is completely fulfilled, it will bring the entire universe into conformity with God.

Most of us think somewhat mystically about heaven. Though the Bible gives only glimpses of its glory, it clearly tells us that God intends to do away completely with the existing world and make an entirely new heaven and a new earth.

- But the day of the Lord will come as a thief in the night; in the which the heavens shall pass away with a great noise, and the elements shall melt with fervent heat, the earth also and the works that are therein will be burned up. . . . Nevertheless we, according to His promise, look for new heavens and a new earth, wherein dwelleth righteousness (2 Pet. 3:10–13).
- For our conversation is in heaven; from whence also we look for the Savior, the Lord Jesus Christ: Who

shall change our vile body, that it may be fashioned like unto his glorious body (Phil. 3:20–21).

- And God shall wipe away all tears from their eyes; and there shall be no more death, neither sorrow, nor crying, neither shall there be any more pain: for the former things are passed away (Rev. 21:4).

There is, of course, much more to heaven than we could ever grasp in this dying world. Maybe that is why God did not tell us more. As humans, we would probably be unable to visualize or even appreciate what God has in store for us (Eph. 2:7). What He *did* want us to know (and to believe) was that He is going to completely restore the creation and that we will live with Him there (John 14:1–4; Rev. 21:3–5).

How Then, Should We Interpret Scripture?

Given all that God has done to convey who He is and what He wants us to know, how should we approach His Word? How can we, with our fallen minds, understand His holy communication? What method can we use that would bring us most carefully before His written word? Is there such a process? Can the mind of man privately decide?

Perhaps the best "process" is the one with the least human involvement. Surely, the God of our salvation knows our limits. Surely, the One who has caused His revealed Word to be recorded knows how to communicate with us. Are we trying to foist a fallible system on that which God has inspired? Do we, by our scholarship, filter the life out of the Word? Are we, by our science, polluting the pure milk of God's Word? Given what we know about ourselves and about our amazing universe, what more respect and honor can we give to the Bible than to simply believe its words?

Isaiah tells us that God's knowledge and doctrine is built "precept . . . upon precept, precept upon precept; line upon line, line upon line; here a little and there a little" (Isa. 28:9–10). Solomon teaches that the wise preacher gave knowledge to the people when he "gave good heed, and sought out, and set in order many proverbs. The preacher sought to find out acceptable words: and that which was written was upright, even words of truth" (Eccles. 12:9–10). Peter insists that the words of God were not of private interpretation (2 Pet. 1:20) and that the "great and precious promises" of God's word are sufficient for "life and godliness" (2 Pet. 1:3-4). Given what is so obviously taught about the precision and accuracy of God's words, should we not be very careful about what we add to or take away from those words?

Perhaps the *best* interpretation is the least interpretation.

To be Berean, remember God's words:

For my thoughts are not your thoughts,
neither are your ways my ways,
saith the Lord.
For as the heavens are higher than the earth,
So are my ways higher than your ways,
And my thoughts than your thoughts.
— Isaiah 55:8–9

Trust in the Lord with all thine heart;
and lean not unto thine own understanding.
In all thy ways acknowledge him,
And he shall direct thy paths.
— Proverbs 3:5–6

Endnotes

1 Fr. Seraphim Rose, *Genesis, Creation, and Early Man* (Platina, CA: St. Herman of Alaska Brotherhood, 2000), p. 24, quoting Fr. Seraphim Rose in editor's preface.
2 Charles Templeton, *Farewell to God* (Toronto: McClelland & Stewart Inc., 1996), p. 232.
3 Dan Barker, *Losing Faith In Faith* (Madison, WI: Freedom From Religion Foundation, Inc., 1992), p. 28–31.

Suggested Reading

This bibliography has been assembled for those who might like to explore more detailed information or scientific apologetic than has been the scope of this book. Many of these books, although in print for some time, remain as classic foundations for the scientific arguments in favor of a young earth and a global flood. Many other titles remain in print to meet the needs of various age groups and different technical disciplines. Addresses of the three main creationist organizations are at the end of this bibliography.

Astronomy and Cosmology

Humphreys, D. Russell. *Starlight and Time.* Green Forest, AR: Master Books, 1994.

DeYoung, Don B. *Astronomy and Creation an Introduction.* St. Joseph, MO: Creation Research Society Books, 1995.

DeYoung, Don B., and Emmett L. Williams, eds. *Design and Origins in Astronomy,* Vol. 2. St. Joseph, MO: Creation Research Society Books, 2002.

Mulfinger, George, Jr. *Design and Origins in Astronomy,* Vol. 1. St. Joseph, MO: Creation Research Society Books, 1996.

Geology, the Genesis Flood, and the Age of the Earth

Morris, Henry M., and John C. Whitcomb. *The Genesis Flood.* Phillipsburg, NJ: Presbyterian and Reformed, 1961.

Morris, John D. *The Young Earth.* Green Forest, AR: Master Books, 1994.

Vardiman, Larry, Andrew A. Snelling, and Eugene F. Chaffin, eds. *Radioisotopes and the Age of the Earth.* Institute for Creation Research and Creation Research Society, 2000.

Woodmorappe, John. *The Mythology of Modern Dating Methods.* El Cajon, CA: Institute for Creation Research, 1999.

General Creation Science

Ashton, John F., ed. *On the Seventh Day.* Green Forest, AR: Master Books, 2002.

Bird, W. R. *The Origin of Species Revisited.* 2 vols. New York: Philosophical Library, 1989.

Gish, Duane T. *Amazing Story of Creation.* El Cajon, CA: Institute for Creation Research, 1990.

Ham, Ken. *Genesis and the Decay of the Nations.* Green Forest, AR: Master Books, 1991.

———. *The Lie Evolution.* Ken Ham Green Forest, AR: Master Books, 1987.

Ham, Ken, and Jonathan Sarfati, and Carl Wieland. *The Revised and Expanded Answers Book.* Edited by Don Batten. Green Forest, AR: Master Books, 1990.

Johnson, Phillip E. *Darwin on Trial.* 2nd ed. Downers Grove, IL: InterVarsity Press, 1993.

Lubenow, Marvin L. *Bones of Contention: A Creationist Assessment of Human Fossils.* Grand Rapids, MI: Baker Books, 1992.

Morris, Henry M. *Scientific Creationism.* Green Forest, AR: Master Books, 1985.

———. *That Their Words May Be Used Against Them.* Institute for Creation Research and Master Books, 1997.

Morris, Henry M., and John D. Morris. *The Modern Creation Trilogy.* 3 Vols. Green Forest, AR: Master Books, 1996.

Morris, John. *Is the Big Bang Biblical?* Green Forest, AR: Master Books, 2003.

Morris, John, and Steven A. Austin. *Footprints in the Ash.* Green Forest, AR: Master Books, 2003.

Parker, Gary. *Creation: Facts of Life.* Green Forest, AR: Master Books, 1994.

Sarfati, Jonathan. *Refuting Evolution.* Green Forest, AR: Master Books, 1999.

———. *Refuting Evolution 2.* Green Forest, AR: Master Books, 2002.

Sunderland, Luther. *Darwin's Enigma: Ebbing the Tide of Naturalism.* Green Forest, AR: Master Books, 1998.

Biblical Commentaries

Morris, Henry M. *The Biblical Basis for Modern Science.* Green Forest, AR: Master Books, 2002.

———. *The Genesis Record.* Grand Rapids, MI: Baker Book House,1976.

———. *The Long War Against God.* Green Forest, AR: Master Books,2000.

Secular Authors

Behe, Michael J. *Darwin's Black Box.* New York: Touchstone Books/Simon and Schuster, 1996.

Denton, Michael. *Evolution: A Theory in Crisis.* Chevy Chase, MD: Adler & Adler, 1986.

Scripture Index

The Institute for Creation Research
P.O. Box 2667
El Cajon, CA 92021
www.icr.org

Other Creationist Organizations
Answers in Genesis
[illegible]
Florence, KY 41022
www.answersingenesis.org

The Creation Research Society
(Professional Membership Society)
P.O. Box 8663
St. Joseph, MO 64508
www.creationresearch.org